GW00372768

Addenda

A number of changes to the text of *Then and Now* were made by the author during rehearsal and after the play was printed. They are given here and should be incorporated into future productions.

p.77 line 7 now reads: *'A Mozart horn concerto is playing softly, near the end. The needle clicks in the track.'*

p.77 line 11. After 'Touché', FENWICK *turns off the record.*

p.80 line 19. JOHN says 'Sir —', after ISABEL's line: 'Daddy — John Baildon.'

p.81 line 23. Delete: *'The Mozart has stopped.'*

p.93 line 4. Delete: 'Agnostic in all things. A wild one.'

p.93 line 26. Delete: *'then puts it away in a drawer. She sits looking into the fire.'*

p.101 line 19. Delete: '. . . however insincere'

p.107 line 17. Delete   'EMMA.   I wonder how he got rich enough to afford you?' Insert: 'EMMA.   I thought you only did women.
                   JOHN.   There was a bit of a foul-up, somewhere.
                   EMMA.   Will he be able to afford you?'

p.111 line 24. Instead of 'Do you care?', JOHN says: 'Well I nearly did. Does it matter?'

p.111 line 31. Instead of 'Three hernias', JOHN says: 'Three D & C's'

p.112 line 15. Delete: 'to you'. JOHN now says: 'And what makes you think I'm coming back?'

p.112 last line. After *'Pause'*, add: 'ROBERT *switches off the music.'*

p.115 line 4. After 'Yes please', ISABEL *turns on the horn concerto — softly.*

p.115 line 15. After 'It goes everywhere with me', ISABEL *switches the music off.*

p.115 line 20 now reads '. . . figurine over there? *(He looks the wrong way.)* Over there.'

p.115 line 22. Instead of 'Mycenean', ISABEL says 'Etruscan'.

p.118 line 29 now reads 'JOHN *and* ISABEL *enter together, she in a chic suit and hat.'*

p.119 line 23. After 'Yes. I had him yesterday', JOHN *switches off the music.*

p.127. Stage direction at the beginning of Scene Four now reads: ISABEL's *apartment. Late the following night.* ISABEL *enters in a black dress and looking haggard — with* ROBERT.

p.129 line 21. ISABEL's line now reads: 'If that figurine weren't too precious, I'd split your skull with it.'

p.131 line 17. ROBERT — after *'Pause'* — now says: 'But I don't know. How she and John —'

p.132 line 9 now reads: *'He goes out. After a moment* ISABEL *picks up her glass and sits hunched forward on the settee, expressionless.'*

p.132 line 18 now reads: '. . . *kisses the top of her head. Gives her a package of perfume.'*

The cast for the Hampstead Theatre production, which opened on 21 May 1979, was Mike Gwilym (JOHN), Liz Smith (MRS BAILDON), John Nettleton (FENWICK), Morag Hood (ISABEL), Patricia Hodge (EMMA) and Simon Chandler (ROBERT). The play was directed by Robin Lefevre.

The Monster of Karlovy Vary & Then and Now

This double volume contains David Mercer's two new stage plays: *The Monster of Karlovy Vary*, published prior to production, and *Then and Now*, first staged at Hampstead Theatre in May 1979.

The Monster of Karlovy Vary is a black farce set in present day Czechoslovakia and revolving around the plight of one, Horatio Dander, who finds that he has been hired by mistake as a screenwriter for a grotesque international co-production which never gets off the ground. The pace is fast and furious, the political satire incisive, and the writing witty and inventive. *The Monster* is something of a departure for David Mercer, but he conducts the farcical proceedings as to the manner born.

Reviewing *Then and Now* in Hampstead, John Elsom described it as a 'story of hopes that went wrong, loves lost and missions unaccomplished. The first act ends optimistically, in the last months of the Second World War, as John Baildon, a miner's son making good, riotously celebrates VE night, with Isabel Fenwick, the niece of a lord, in a room at Claridges. Isobel wants life after the war to return to normal, John is determined that Britain must change; but both are happy, drunk and, within limits of which they know nothing, free. The second act is about what is happening to them today . . .

'*Then and Now*, Mercer's best play for many years, works on the level of contrasts — not between good and bad, or even hope and despair, but between two cultures, one emerging from the other, both with their strengths and weaknesses. It is an ambiguous play, with ironies built into the fabric of the text, each line reflecting or anticipating another, with no strong conclusions drawn.'

(*The Listener*)

The photograph of David Mercer on the back cover is reproduced by courtesy of Irving Teitelbaum.

David Mercer

THE MONSTER OF KARLOVY VARY
&
THEN AND NOW

A722572

AVON COUNTY LIBRARY

– 4 FEB 1980

Class No. DR

Alloc. | Suppl, French

EYRE METHUEN · LONDON

First published in 1979 by Eyre Methuen Ltd
11 New Fetter Lane, London EC4P 4EE
Copyright © 1979 by David Mercer
Set in IBM 10 point Journal by 🔫 Tek-Art Croydon, Surrey
Printed by Whitstable Litho Ltd. Whitstable, Kent

ISBN 0 413 46210 2

All rights whatsoever in these plays are strictly reserved and
application for performance, etc., should be made before rehearsal
to Margaret Ramsay Ltd., 14a Goodwin's Court, London WC2N
4LL. No performance may be given unless a licence has been
obtained.

This paperback edition is sold subject to the condition that it
shall not, by way of trade or otherwise, be lent, resold, hired out,
or otherwise circulated without the publisher's prior consent in
any form of binding or cover other than that in which it is
published and without a similar condition including this condition
being imposed on the subsequent purchaser.

THE MONSTER OF KARLOVY VARY

Characters

HORATIO DANDER, *a screenwriter*
JIŘÍ KLINKA, *a film director*
GUSTAV TURP, *a film producer*
LUDMILA KLINKOVÁ, *an actress and Klinka's wife*
MILAN HÁJEK, *a bureaucrat*
JANA, *Klinka's assistant*
JAROSLAV KLUMM, *a secret agent*
MILOŠ, *a driver*
KRK, *a bureaucrat*
KLÁRA, *Krk's assistant*
LOUIS BEANEY, *a film director*
HEINI DINDL, *Horatio's father*

WAITERS, SECRET POLICEMEN and OTHERS.

Act One

Scene One

Barrandov Film Studios in Prague. Time the present. A film camera. A fierce blaze from clustered lights. JIŘÍ KLINKA stands peering through the camera viewer. He is a handsome paunchy man in his sixties with grey receding hair.

KLINKA (*in Czech*). Cut! Horrible! Terrible!

> *The lights are doused. KLINKA slumps into a canvas chair and stares at his feet. Taps one foot nervously. Lights a thin cigar. Takes a red balloon from one pocket and blows it up. He sits looking at it, then explodes it with the tip of his cigar.*
> *His assistant JANA enters with HORATIO DANDER, an Englishman in his mid-twenties. DANDER approaches KLINKA nervously.*

JANA. Pan Klinka — Pan Dander. Mr Dander — Jiří Klinka.

KLINKA (*in Czech*). Who?

JANA. Your English writer, just now arrived from London.

KLINKA. Dander? Him?

DANDER. Yes. Horatio.

KLINKA. There's a strong vein of fantastic humour in my films Dander. You look like a solemn little bastard to me.

DANDER. It's only skin deep. I hope you were expecting me. Turp said he'd wire you from London.

KLINKA (*snaps his fingers. JANA gives him a telegram*). Horatio. (*Pause.*) Maybe I call you Whore-ratio — huh?

DANDER. People have in their time.

KLINKA (*reading*). Turp refers to you as a script doctor. This is whoring — no?

DANDER. Well anyway I can write.

KLINKA. So? So whores can screw.

DANDER. I think I might be high-class courtesan material.

KLINKA. According to Turp you won an award. It's true?

DANDER. For a play.

KLINKA. Royal Court? National Theatre? Royal Shakespeare Company?

DANDER. Children's television.

KLINKA. It all fits.

DANDER. I must admit. I do think writing awards are immoral.

KLINKA. Shrewd boy. (*He waves the telegram.*) Listen. If Gustav Turp is telling the truth, it has to be an item unworthy of his talent for lying. You have an agent? He must be crazy.

DANDER. He is crazy.

KLINKA. Dander. Are you clear about where you are?

Pause.

DANDER. Prague.

KLINKA (*waves the telegram*). Turp is a crook, a phoney and a philistine.

DANDER. I know.

KLINKA. Shrewd boy.

DANDER. Still. He's paying me a hundred a week to do the English version of your screenplay.

KLINKA. Has he paid you anything yet?

DANDER. Not exactly.

KLINKA. Signed a contract?

DANDER. No.

KLINKA. He won't.

DANDER. I'll do it for nothing.

KLINKA. You already are.

DANDER. I have a few ideas about what went wrong, Mr Klinka.

KLINKA. You have the nerve to criticise my script?

DANDER. I was thinking more of the Bolshevik Revolution.

KLINKA (*to* JANA). Get him on the next plane to London. (*To* DANDER.) Call me Jirka. (*Going close.*) So what do we have here? The infantile left? A marxist playboy of the western world?

DANDER. Not precisely.

KLINKA. What are you precisely?

DANDER. Well. (*Pause.*) What about: worried armchair revolutionary?

KLINKA. Yes? I don't like it.

DANDER. I felt obliged to come and have a look, anyway.

KLINKA. At Czechoslovakia?

DANDER. I thought one should —

KLINKA. See how the patient's getting along?

DANDER. I wouldn't presume.

KLINKA (*moving away*). Turp always was a sadist.

DANDER. He's done me no harm. Yet.

KLINKA. I speak, my dear boy, of what he's doing to me.

DANDER. By hiring me?

KLINKA. You think we can have marxists running around loose in this country?

DANDER. I'd have thought —

KLINKA. Don't think, mein Lieber. Pack. (*He grinds out his cigar — puts his hands on* DANDER'S *shoulders.*) My dear. Looking into your beautiful blue eyes. Where did the obscene Turp find you?

DANDER. He rang my agent. Said he was a producer making an anglo-Czech film, and —

KLINKA. Needed the latest genius? Mentioned your name? Offered peanuts?

DANDER. I imagine that was about the drift of it.

KLINKA. You don't know about Gus Turp?

DANDER. I'd never heard of him.

KLINKA. Did your agent have some special reason for getting you out of England, Horatio? Debts? Paternity orders? You been standing on somebody's toes? Publicly insulted the Arts Council?

DANDER. As far as I know, my agent thinks I've been boringly inoffensive all round.

KLINKA *puts his arm paternally round* DANDER'S *shoulders and starts walking him up and down.*

KLINKA. Apart from a few wretches like me, Turp is unknown to the world at large. At the same time he's everywhere: London, Hollywood, New York, Rome, Paris. At all the film festivals from Sao Paulo to Moskva. And whilst having the unique faculty of seeming to be in all places at more or less the same time, he is in some respects invisible. (*Finds a cigar.*) What do I mean? It's as if nobody sees Turp. There he is, on the beach at Cannes. Dinners, receptions, awards ceremonies. Turp in permanent orbit round the great and powerful of the film world. And you know what? He's there, but people pass through him. He's been passed through — dammit as if he were made of air — by all the promenading kings of Metro, Fox, United Artists, Columbia. It's as if the very molecules of Turp's body part like the waters of the Red Sea. And the high and mighty go through this small fat hysterical producer as if he would be a cobweb. (*Gripping* DANDER'S *arm.*) When here at Barrandov we come to a foreign co-production like virgins to a pimp — who scuttles along? Who's in there fighting? Yes. Turp. (*Walks on, hugging* DANDER'S *shoulders.*) 'Old Gus' as he likes to be called when feeling sycophantic. And what's he got? What's his virtue, his talent? He's the only one to come forward and take a chance. Why not? He's been bankrupt most of his life. (*Pause.*) But I have to tell you Dander. I admire him for it. I do. In the West you may have Polanski. You may have Forman and Passer. But we have Turp. (*Grinds out his cigar.*) I have Turp. (*Pause.*) One thing I will say for the events of sixty-eight. The real talent got out of the country leaving the field wide open at last for Klinka. (*Grips* DANDER, *staring at him.*) Your agent didn't put you wise?

DANDER. I think my agent thought Old Gus was somebody else.

KLINKA. What a sonofabitch handing a baby in arms to that shyster! You're out of your class, Horatio. Go back to writing for the kiddies, will you? I can see you think you've got a mind of your own. In this country it's dynamite. They'll fry me. You think Cechoslovakia's a tragedy? It's worse. It's a land of opportunity for people like me and Turp. (*Shakes* DANDER *till his teeth rattle.*) Go home, little Sheba! (*Embraces him and steps back.*) I tell you what. Jana — (*She hurries forward.*) Take Mr Dander back to his hotel. Show him the town. Turp flies in tomorrow, we put the boy in the same plane back to London. Practise your English. Play him your punk records. Fill him with slivovitz.

JANA. Yes, Mr Klinka.

KLINKA. Try not to give him the heave-ho. Keep him out of trouble, know what I mean?

JANA. Yes, Mr Klinka.

KLINKA. Only by the way —

JANA. Sir?

KLINKA. You screw him, I'll have you pumping petrol somewhere in the Tatras Mountains. You understand?

JANA. I do.

KLINKA (*to* DANDER). You read my humble screenplay?

DANDER. In the plane from London.

KLINKA. It's shit — no?

DANDER. Absolute crap. Naive. Sentimental. Old-fashioned. (*Pause.*) Awful.

KLINKA. Shrewd boy.

He goes. DANDER *smiles shyly at* JANA — *who sits in* KLINKA'S *chair — and stands looking round.*

DANDER. I've never been in a film studio before.

JANA. What would you like to do in Prague, Mr Dander?

DANDER. Please call me Horatio.

JANA. It makes me giggle. How could your parents do it to you?

DANDER. Ah well. Mother was Argentinian. I'm told Horacio sounds okay in Buenos Aires. Not that I ever knew her. Babyhood shrouded in mystery, and so on. Posted to England like a wee parcel at the age of two. Raised in loco parentis by one of those nannies. She crackled, as she bowled me along in my pushchair. Must have been the starch. She told me father went to build a factory in Hong Kong and was never seen again. I suspect the bugger's in the land of the rising sun. Every month for twenty years till I came down from Oxford I had an allowance through a legal firm in Tokyo. Exotic, if enigmatic. (*Pause.*) I like to think that father gave up the things of this world and sits on a Japanese mountain preparing for the next.

JANA. Poor Horacio. All alone —

DANDER. Not quite. I have my agent. Sometimes I have the feeling he could almost be my mother in drag.

KLINKA *re-enters wearing a rather chic anorak and a Brechtian cap. He fumbles at a cigar with a gold lighter.*

KLINKA. On second thoughts, Dander —

DANDER (*primly*). Rejection is the mother of remorse.

KLINKA (*tenderly to* JANA). I was just like him at his age.

DANDER. Are you suggesting I shall be just like you at yours?

KLINKA. Horatio, my wife's just been screaming at me. When she screams I feel humble. I stood there feeling humble and the expression on my face felt just like the one I'd seen on yours. I'm sorry, my boy. It isn't good enough to hand over a foreigner and honoured guest to this female piranha without a by-your-leave. I fixed you two an official car and chauffeur for the evening. Use it. Keep him up till all hours. He makes more than I do, and it rankles. He's a good driver and a dedicated informer. (*He fingers* DANDER'S *lapel.*) But a word of caution, mein Lieber —

DANDER. Yes?

KLINKA *seizes* JANA *and kisses her noisily on both cheeks.*

KLINKA. So is little Jana here. I surround myself with them. It's an infallible method for taking wind out of the official sails, and leaves me knowing where I stand. (*Hugging* JANA *carelessly.*) In her case where I lie.

DANDER. I must say, I admire your English.

KLINKA. I was with the RAF during the war. Seems only last week. (*Shakes* DANDER'S *forearm.*) I like you, Dander. Was your pater with the Brylcreem boys?

DANDER. Rumour had it (*to* JANA) — Nanny again — (*to* KLINKA) he was a tail gunner in the Luftwaffe.

KLINKA. There you are. Turp *is* trying to destroy me.

DANDER. Well I certainly hope dad never fired on you.

KLINKA. I was shooting film you idiot, not people. Nobody told me you're a godamn kraut, by the way. Danderle? Danderlein? It doesn't figure.

DANDER. No no no. You've got it all wrong. Well nearly. What I am is a sort of triumph of the environment over the genes. English through and through in that respect. Prep school in Hampstead. Seven years at the London Lycée. Three at Oxford. And also by the way, 'it doesn't figure' is an American expression. One of many you seem addicted to, such as: 'like he was' instead of 'as if he were'. Your screenplay's riddled with them.

KLINKA. I'll have you hung from the yard arm.

DANDER. Hanged.

KLINKA. How — might one ask? How were you translated from the balls of a tail-gunner in the Luftwaffe to a prep school in Hampstead?

DANDER. It's obscure. I'm still shuffling the historical pieces. Getting it together, (*primly*) as we say nowadays.

KLINKA. Shuffling the — history isn't some kind of bloody kaleidoscope! History is —

JANA. Pane Klinka —

KLINKA. Now what?

JANA (*archly*). Pas devant les capitalistes, Maître.

KLINKA. So? So what about Turp? Old Gus is playing poker with the historical pieces. Doesn't he exemplify capitalism's very contradictions?

DANDER. Bravo!

JANA. Mr Turp — objectively speaking — is assisting us in the task of capital accumulation.

KLINKA. You hear that Dander?

DANDER. It's on the brink of plausibility.

KLINKA. It's the little nightmare's way of flirting with me. It's her tiresome notion of ideological fun. (*Pulls* JANA'S *nose.*) What a long way the child's come. Before she joined the Party they used to call her Darkness at Noon, hereabouts. Well, there you go Dander. There it is. Prague is yours for a night. That's nearly as long as we've had it ourselves. (*Clenched fist salute.*) Avanti, populi! Got to finish that screaming session. You have my screenplay there?

DANDER *takes the screenplay from a flat zippered briefcase.* KLINKA *grabs it and rips it to pieces, throwing the bits up in the air.*

Okay. So I'm not Bergman. I'm not Buñuel. I'm not fit to lick Fellini's boots, huh?

DANDER. I'm glad you've come to terms with it Jirka.

KLINKA. Jana ring Turp's office in London and tell him I want Pinter. Ring Souček and tell him I've got Pinter. Ring Bohumil

and tell him Souček's got Pinter. Bohumil objects — he's an
anti-semite. (*Turning on* DANDER.) On no account will I have
this Dander. He smells like he was trouble. 'As if he were'
trouble. Okay, Dander?

He goes. DANDER *gazes thoughtfully at* JANA.

DANDER. Are you really an informer?

JANA. That's what seems to keep everybody happy. (*She moves
in seductively.*) I once had a teddy-bear called Míška Medvídek.
May I call you Misha, Horacio?

DANDER. I wish it to go on record that I'm highly shocked by
almost everything I hear.

JANA. It already has.

DANDER. D'you think he needs any help? Where do he and his
wife do their screaming?

JANA. Stage three, dressing room one.

DANDER. She's a film star?

JANA. You've never heard of Ludmila Klinková? She's the Faye
Dunaway of the People's Democracies, Mr Dander.

DANDER. Misha, if you like.

JANA. Misha.

Pause.

DANDER. I never imagined it would be like this.

JANA (*bows mockingly*). Prague is at your feet, Sir.

DANDER. The truth of the matter is, Jana. When I pondered
this adventure at Heathrow Airport . . . sitting there with my
asbestos sandwich and a cup of dogsweat —

JANA. You need someone, I can tell.

DANDER. The truth is. I had a little subversion in mind.

JANA. You had the fantasy to blow up Terminal Two?

DANDER. Er — I was thinking more of the terminal regime over
here.

Pause. She takes his arm.

JANA (*leading him off*). Do you know what happened to a
famous Czech called Jan Hus, Misha?

Fade out.

Scene Two

A small cellar club in Prague, the same night.

There are two or three tables. A thin clientele of young people in jeans and sneakers. The place is dim and smoky. Loudspeakers play some tight formal jazz which should not be danced to – but DANDER *and* JANA *stand swaying together gently.*

The track changes. They go to a table, where they have a bottle of wine.

DANDER. Isn't this place a wee bit on the decadent side?

JANA. The normalisation programme has many angles, Misha.

DANDER. I was under the impression the country was just one damn big prison.

JANA. Then perhaps you'll find a little decadence reassuring.

DANDER. One of my tutors at Oxford was a Czech. (*Pause.*) I directed a neat little play of his, called *Who's Afraid of the Good Soldier Schweik?* Marvellous ending. The entire Red Army up to its neck in a bog.

JANA. Mockery, Misha, is the lowest form of treachery.

DANDER. Would you betray me? Klinka? Who's your filthy boss?

JANA. Please don't use that ugly word 'betrayal'. We call it 'data processing'. What's more, we try to protect people like you. It's one of the rules of the game at the Ministry of the Interior. (*She fumbles in her bag and shows him a photo.*)

DANDER. Not a bad likeness.

JANA. It's you in immigration control at the airport. It was lying on my desk this afternoon with a note from what you rudely call my 'filthy boss' saying – roughly translated from the Czech – guard this dummkopf with your life.

DANDER. He drew in the wings and halo, the bastard?

JANA. He was in a frivolous mood. He'd just been reading your ex-tutor's play. (*Takes photo back, smiling.*) They have it on file at our embassy in London. (*Sips wine.*) My boss thinks the Schweikian tendency in Czech history has been much exaggerated. It's the sort of pathetic straw, he says, that the liberal Western mind clings to. (*Sips.*) It was he who instructed Customs to overlook your gun, in case you'd wondered.

Pause.

DANDER. I'd hoped the Lego box would fool them.

JANA. Silly boy. It's a craze over here just now. If they hadn't been so intrigued by the gun they'd have confiscated the Lego like a shot. Which Lego was it?

DANDER. The red indians in the canoe and the squaw with the papoose.

JANA. Klinka has that one in his office. (*Pause.*) And what exactly had you in mind with the gun? According to our man at Customs, the barrel's packed solid with chocolate.

DANDER. An exaggeration. It's marzipan. Took me hours. What had I in mind? I thought I might need something a bit more impressive than indignation, over here.

A WAITER *brings a telephone on a long flex. He bends to whisper in* JANA'S *ear and gives her the receiver.*

JANA. Hello. Yes. (*Pause.*) One moment, please. (*She hands it to* DANDER.) Your agent in London.

DANDER. How amazing.

JANA. Not at all. I inform the exchange where we are and they switch any calls through from your hotel.

DANDER. My agent amazing I mean. Getting through at all. He's convinced Prague's the capital of Bulgaria.

JANA. He's already tried Budapest and Warsaw.

DANDER. Hello? Nathaniel? (*Pause.*) No. Listen. (*Pause.*) What do you mean? (*Pause.*) In a sort of club. What? She's Klinka's assistant. Moonlights in the secret police. That's right. Looking after me —

He pours wine into a glass, lights a cigarette, all the time holding the phone away from his ear. It squawks audibly. After a moment he sets it down and rises.

Excuse me a moment.

JANA (*pointing at the phone*). What about —

DANDER. It's all right. Leave it there. I'm just going for a pee.

He goes. JANA *picks up the phone and listens. She takes a notebook from her bag and starts writing. When* DANDER *reappears she puts the phone back on the table.*

JANA. Don't you ever listen to him?

DANDER. Would you if your agent talks about nothing but his

other writers? He never even seems to realise it's me he's talking to. The other day his secretary put him through to me and he said: Am I ringing you or are you ringing me? You're ringing me Nathaniel I said. Well Mac he said, I just wanted to tell you that new script of yours is fantastic. Witty, elegant — it's all muscle Mac. Not an ounce of fat. Keep it up sweetheart.

They both gaze at the recumbent still squawking phone.

JANA (*peers at her notebook*). Well it seems this time an American TV company rang about a series of half-hour plays on — (*Peering.*) great dictators in history.

DANDER. What? A whole wicked life in half an hour?

JANA. Yes and they're offering Stalin to somebody called McPherson for twenty-thousand dollars.

DANDER (*grabbing the phone*). Nathaniel? Natty? McPherson here. Aye, Mcpherrrson. Shut up and listen, will you? I accept you fool. (*Long pause.*) Natty? (*Rattles miserably at the cradle and puts the phone down.*) His last words were: I gave it to them straight Mac. My authors are not interested in money and that's final. (*Pause.*) I could weep. I'm ashamed to say I might even have licked Stalin's boots for twenty-thousand dollars.

JANA. You'd be in good company round here. But a bit pricey.

DANDER. It's all right for Natty Bunce. He casts us in roles and we're supposed to live up to them. McPherson's the dark austere genius. Driscoll's the true incorruptible. Me I'm the feckless foundling, a sucker for anybody that waves a rattle and shouts coochi-coochi. Bunce has four terrific money-spinners, and the rest of us are supposed to be above it all. Coming from a man whose grandparents made a fortune out of ostrich feathers in South Africa it leaves one a bit sullen. When the boa went out, so did the Bunce fortune — but he's made up for it. I mean. You can see the clear line from feathers to show-business. (*Drinks.*) I wonder what the bankrupt Bunces did with ten thousand redundant ostriches?

JANA (*smiles, raising her glass*). Coochi-coochi.

There is a slow roll of drums from the loudspeakers. The lights dim. Silence.

DANDER. It'd better be audacious, that's all I can say. I've got to run into trouble somehow, before I leave.

*A blackout. A long slow crescendo of male voices singing the
'Horst Wessel' song. The sound of marching feet, rhythmic and
insistent*

*The song reaches its climax as a spotlight fades up on a male
figure with a matt white clown's face lying huddled in a black
cloak.*

*The song fades. Massed choirs singing the 'Internationale' take
its place. As the music slowly swells, the cloaked figure mimes
a slow and painful resurrection. This and the following mime
should be as moving as possible.*

At the climax of the 'Internationale' the CLOWN *throws off
his cloak joyfully and stands revealed in a leotard harlequin-
patterned in Czech national colours.*

The music changes to Dvořak's 'New World Symphony'. The
CLOWN *dances joy and liberty.*

There is a sudden burst of submachine-gun fire. The CLOWN
freezes.

Two DANCERS *in olive-green tights and the jackets and caps
of Red Army soldiers dance round the* CLOWN *to the sound
of the national anthem. They bind his eyes and mouth with
red bandanas, his wrists and ankles with red wooden manacles.
Now the* CLOWN *performs a ghastly parody of the Dvořak
mime, sadly encumbered by his bonds. As the music dies away
he freezes in a crouching position of bondage.*

*A blackout. The blare of police car sirens. In the darkness
there is a great deal of scuffling and shouting. Furniture
breaking, howls of pain, the thud of blows.*

When the lights come on the place is wrecked and deserted.
DANDER *sits on the floor rubbing the back of his neck. One
of his coat sleeves is practically torn from the shoulder.* JANA,
*very cool and unruffled, kneels beside him pressing a napkin
to a cut on his cheek.*

*An open door bangs somewhere. A wind blows through the
cellar.* JANA *helps* DANDER *to his feet and gives him a drink.
He looks round at the desolate scene.*

JANA. Satisfied?

DANDER. Well. That was a bit more like it. That was fairly up to
scratch. I've a splendid feeling I smashed somebody's nose.
(*Dusting himself down.*) That's definitely a bit more bloody
like it. Do you think they were arrested, poor sods? Heroes one
and all.

JANA. No. They've been flown to Moscow to receive the Order
of Lenin.

DANDER. Sarcasm's a pretty low form of treachery too, you know. (*Rubbing the back of his head.*) I took a fair crack on the head myself, as a matter of fact. (*Pause: looks round.*) At grips with brutal tyranny at last —

JANA. I could almost fall in love with you, Misha.

DANDER. Would the Ministry of the Interior approve?

JANA. Why not? You should hear my boss on the subject of the dialectical fuck.

DANDER *faints*. JANA *calls out*.

Miloš? (*Pause.*) Miloš —

MILOŠ *the driver enters: a grey-haired kindly looking man of sixty in a red and black lumber-jacket and a brown leather flat cap. He swings DANDER effortlessly over his shoulder and goes out followed by JANA.*
Fade out.

Fade in.

Scene Three

JANA'S *room in Prague, the same night.*
  JANA *enters followed by MILOŠ supporting DANDER. MILOŠ helps DANDER into a chair and slips off his torn jacket. He takes out a hip flask and fills the cap, offering it to DANDER.*
  JANA *finds a sewing basket and begins to repair the jacket.*

MILOŠ. Throw it back in one go, Pane Dander.

DANDER *does so. It shakes him rigid.*

My own brew. I used to have a little shack in the country a few years back. Had a still in the henhouse. (*Pause.*) You've had a rough time — what about another? (DANDER *proffers the cap and MILOŠ refills it, stands sniffing the bottle.*) Add one of these to a hundred grams of cherry brandy. A dash of bourbon. A splash of soda, and you've got a real humdinger. What I used to call a 'Beria' in the bad old days. (*Sighs.*) In the better old days it fell into disrepute even as a drink.

DANDER (*nodding at JANA*). I wouldn't get nostalgic about anything at all in front of her. If I were you.

MILOŠ. I don't give a bugger who I offend any more. (*Takes a long pull.*) Not since we got our logical democracy. (*Ticks off fingers.*) I've been a lumberjack, a waiter, a bricklayer, a roadmender. Driving for Pan Klinka's a step in the upward direction, you might say. (*Leaning forward emphatically.*) The nuances are a bit hard to divine.

DANDER. She's listening to every word —

MILOŠ. And why not, with such a charming pair of ears? (*Drinks.*) We've got two radio-astronomers among the untermensch at the studios. Floorsweepers. (*Cups his ears and hums, moving his head from side to side.*) They call her Jodrell Bank.

DANDER. Dare one ask what you were in the better old days?

MILOŠ. A professor of English up to sixty-nine. Staunch party man from thirty-six. With gaps, you know. (*Drinks.*) Roamed about with the Slovak partisans through the war. Translated *Finnegan's Wake* —

DANDER. Into Czech?

MILOŠ. What else had you in mind? Xhosa? Swahili? (*Drinks.*) Got netted in the wake of the Slánský business. Who didn't? Ten years hard labour. Rehabilitated later than sooner. Always at the back of the queue. A black and bitter business it was, young man. For one who dreamed of communism with a human face long before it became all the rage. (*Pause.*) I should put something on that nasty cut if I were you. (*Looks at* JANA *sewing and turns to* DANDER *with a wink.*) She's doing a neat job, eh? What an all-rounder the woman is.

DANDER. So are you I gather from Klinka.

MILOŠ *presses a finger to the side of his nose and grins.*

MILOŠ. Can you tell me how else I can speak my mind in public and log it up safely as an agent provocateur? (*Drinks.*) It's wonderful to speak English to a genuine limey again.

DANDER. I was going to criticise your position but I haven't the nerve. I don't think I've ever been in a logical democracy.

MILOŠ. The first law of the revolutionary dynamic, Pane Dander — is that mediocrity smacks its lips and bides its time. Then it rushes in when the fools have done the dirty work of murdering the angels. (*Drinks.*) Mediocrity knows its destiny is somewhere at the top. Who was the revolution for, it asks itself? It bites its fingernails. Gets paranoid and envious. Does its egalitarian sums. And hey presto! In the name of ideological

purity your mediocre chap screams and vilifies — grabs the
tanks and the banks with a little assistance from the Kremlin.
And boots those damned humanist intellectuals to the bottom
where they belong. It's logical. It has some of the meaner
characteristics of the democratic idea. Bingo! You have a
logical democracy. (*Drinks.*) Me, I love it at the bottom.
Driving Pan Klinka's the nearest I've ever come to watching
genius burn itself out in a holocaust of self-deception.

DANDER. A genius? Klinka?

MILOŠ. Well. You have to overhaul your terminology a bit in this
country. He's alive. He's well. He's kept out of jail. Still has a
good job and a house. The incredible Ludmila hasn't divorced
him. Two fine children. True they couldn't muster a scruple
between them but never mind it's in the air. (*Drinks.*) Ten to
fifteen thousand crowns a month, and to cap it all Meister
Klinka has Jodrell Bank. Who, they say, makes the Kama
Sutra seem like a boy scouts' manual. If that isn't genius I'm
damned if I know what is. Has she had you yet?

DANDER. Er — no.

MILOŠ (*screwing the cap on the flask*). She will, though. (*Going
out past* JANA.) Won't you Jody? She'll gnaw your knackers
off and send you back to London with Screwed in
Czechoslovakia stamped on your backside. Ahoj, children.

He goes. JANA *holds up the jacket with the sleeve now neatly
stitched to the shoulder. It weighs heavily to one side.* JANA
*feels in the pocket and takes out an automatic pistol. Shakes
her head. Puts it back.*

JANA. What are we going to do with you Misha?

DANDER. I warn you. I'm a virgin.

JANA (*crosses to him, touches his cheek*). Did you bring your
boy scouts' manual? Along with that copy of Gramsci's
prison notebooks?

DANDER. I'll have you know that Gramsci's autographed by
Enrico Berlinguer himself.

JANA. I do know. (*Puts her arms round his neck.*) I've always
wanted a virgin —

DANDER (*disengaging*). Jana. That amazingly cynical driver's
got a very persuasive line, you know. I mean I'm beginning to
think corruption's rife in a situation where strife ought to be
rife. Don't you think? What he says rings dismally true —

JANA. Of course it does Misha. But if you look at it another way, wouldn't it all be equally true of Whitehall or Washington?

DANDER. Dogma says yes, but I think there's a flaw in there somewhere.

JANA. Really, Horacio! I thought you'd have us believe you might be on our side, if only it weren't for our systematic abuse of human rights?

DANDER. Exactly.

JANA. Well it takes time to get people like Miloš out of the security service and back into the community. (*Tartly.*) Where their troubles began in the first place, as your R.D. Laing so witheringly puts it. (*Pause.*) Now Misha. Me — or coffee?

DANDER. Er — where's the bathroom?

JANA (*pointing*). Over there. But I wouldn't —

DANDER. I've got to. Sorry —

As he enters the bathroom there is the eerie glow of a red light from inside. A voice calls 'Get out' in Czech and DANDER *comes out confused.*

There's a man in there developing photos. Who's he? The State pornographer?

The man follows DANDER *out of the bathroom. It is the* CLOWN — *unrecognisable at first without his make-up, and dressed in a white tee-shirt and black trousers. He carries two strips of wet film in clips.*

KLUMM. Dobrý večer —

JANA. This is Mr Jaroslav Klumm, Misha.

DANDER. Dobrý večer, Pan Klumm. Horatio Dander.

KLUMM *re-enters the bathroom.*

DANDER. That face seems familiar. (KLUMM *re-enters, whistling and doing his clown mime.*) It's the clown! (*Pumps* KLUMM'S *hand.*) Mr. Klumm it's an honour. You were terrific. Fantastic. I was so moved I nearly cried. How splendid that you got away.

KLUMM. This the little dummkopf Hájek spoke about?

DANDER. Are you always so rude to your fans?

KLUMM. I work one hour in a red light, it drives me bananas. I can't think of nothing but whores. All shapes and sizes and colours. I get so horny I don't know where to put me.

DANDER. I thought you were in prison.

KLUMM. Me? How could I be in stir?

DANDER. The raid on the club —

KLUMM. Dander. I work for the prison. We ain't started arresting each other yet. That's Stalinism.

DANDER (*to* JANA). How can I stay in the same room?

KLUMM (*miming a camera*). Profile. Full face. Public enemy number five four three two. You know what I mean? Shaved heads. Staring eyes. No time for the elegant shot, the fine angle. (*Approaching* DANDER.) I also get sent to those counter-revolutionary clubs now and then. All righty? (*Grins.*) You and Jody get spliced I'll do your wedding pictures.

He sits astride a chair, leaning over the back. DANDER *crosses to* JANA *for his coat.*

DANDER. You're a disgrace, Klumm. (*Pulling on his jacket.*) You're not worthy of being a fart up a rat's bum, Klumm. (*Making for the door.*)

KLUMM. Just a minute boy. Time to hang up your nuts an' play ball. We got a beaut of you and the broad at tonight's shindig.

DANDER. As far as I'm concerned those people in the café were moral and cultural refugees from tyranny. Or is the whole set-up an extension of the Ministry of the Interior?

KLUMM (*kindly*). What's the worst thing you ever did in your life, Horatio?

Pause. DANDER *is thrown.*

DANDER. I've led a very sheltered life since I left Buenos Aires.

KLUMM (*to* JANA). Buenos Aires? It's him all right.

DANDER. What's me? By the time I was seven and starting to pull myself together ideologically, I was in the grip of the English educational system. Do you know what a progressive Hampstead prep school can do for an otherwise perfectly normal foreigner?

KLUMM. See, Dander. I'm working on these pictures in the john. Now I hear Buenos Aires. Klumm I say to myself — this mugshot's the spit of a geezer I know and love.

DANDER. Which could hardly be anyone I know and love.

KLUMM. Not like say — Heini Dindl?

DANDER *sways.* JANA *has a chair ready and he slowly sinks into it.*

DANDER. Para l'amor de Dios! My father?

KLUMM. We was in the Gestapo together.

DANDER. He was in the Luftwaffe.

KLUMM. Gestapo.

DANDER (*rising*). No father of mine could be in the Gestapo.

KLUMM. You only got one, sonny. No matter what kinda dame your ma was. (*To* JANA.) He's a dead ringer for the old man. Well well well. Old Heini Dindl's kid. Let's drink to it. You got any booze Jana?

DANDER (*pulls out the gun*). Just you take back that lie about my father.

Pause.

KLUMM. Listen. Take it easy. Heini and me was on the run together in forty-five. To Argentina. We split, and I wind up driving a cab in New York. (*Rising.*) Here. Gimme that piece —

DANDER. Sit down. (KLUMM *shrugs and sits.*) You know where my father is?

KLUMM. Still on the lamm, I guess. Who ain't?

DANDER. Are you?

KLUMM. It's like this, cookie. One morning in forty-eight I'm sitting in my cab on fifty-second and Broadway. I'm reading the paper, right? I read they seen the light over here. Out with all that social democratic shit and in with the Party. Masaryk takes a flier off some balcony — I think to myself, Klumm your country needs you.

DANDER. And your act in the club tonight?

KLUMM. You think I can just walk in and take pictures? But you got to admit, Horatio. In the act — I got soul. (*Stands up, spreading his arms.*) Kill me. Go on. Pull the trigger.

DANDER. I will if you don't take back what you said about my father —

Pause.

KLUMM. He was in the Gestapo, sweetheart. Him an' me both.

DANDER *takes a theatrical stance with the gun and pulls the trigger. There is a loud report. A crimson stain blossoms on*

KLUMM'S *shirt and he topples off the chair.* DANDER *is aghast. He stands looking from* KLUMM *to the gun, then kneels with his ear to* KLUMM'S *chest.* JANA *is at the telephone.* DANDER *steps back from the body as she speaks one rapid sentence in Czech, then puts the phone down and goes to* KLUMM. *She listens for his heartbeat.*

DANDER. His heart's still beating.

JANA. Not now it isn't Misha.

DANDER. It's not my gun is it?

JANA. How should I know?

DANDER. And I can't prove it, can I?

JANA. Mr Hájek moves in mysterious ways. His wonders to perform.

DANDER. Who's Hájek?

JANA. My boss. I just rang him.

DANDER *slumps into a chair and sits staring at* KLUMM'S *body.* JANA *gives him a drink.*

DANDER. Can you get Bunce for me in London? Don't tell me you haven't got his number.

JANA. Of course I have.

She finds the number in her notebook and dials. When she gets the London ringing tone she hands the phone to DANDER.

DANDER. Natty? (*Pause.*) Will you just listen a minute? (*Pause.*) Yes I know you think it's McPherson but — (*Lowers the phone sadly, staring at it as it squawks loudly.*) Eleven minutes without stopping is his record with me. I know one famous author of his who said his par for the course is twenty-three. And that's a man with two Oscars. He said he'd only managed to utter two complete sentences on the phone to Natty in eighteen years.

JANA *takes the phone away from him gently and replaces it.*

DANDER. I was going to ask him to get me a lawyer. How quaint of me. (*Crosses to* KLUMM'S *body and touches it with his foot.*) Well. At any rate. I think I've definitely struck a blow for humanism.

MILAN HÁJEK *enters followed by two* HEAVIES *in Russian-style suits.*
HÁJEK *is in his forties: slim, handsome, tanned, very slightly*

camp. He wears a well-cut suit and white polo.

HÁJEK. Mr Dander? (*Shakes hands.*) Don't look so glum. Would
you excuse us for a moment? (*He bends to examine* KLUMM
— *raps out an order in Czech and the* HEAVIES *carry the body
out.*)

DANDER (*holding out the gun*). I've been framed.

HÁJEK. I am sorry. Hájek, by the way. Milan Hájek. Awfully
glad to meet you at last. We've been fascinated by you ever
since you stepped off the plane.

DANDER. I shall insist on a public trial you know.

HÁJEK. Trial? My dear chap there isn't going to be one. I promise
you.

DANDER. There will be when the British Government hears about
this.

HÁJEK. Horatio! Bourgeois justice? You? (*To* JANA.) Jana. Did
you get the wine and that excellent Moravian cheese I had sent
round this morning? Let's have a wee snack and talk things
over.

JANA *proceeds to cover a small table with a checked cloth.
She finds the wine, cheese, glasses, bread.* HÁJEK *will uncork
the wine.*

HÁJEK. After all, I can quite see what our young friend's driving
at. He wants to put the entire regime on trial. Don't you
Horatio? Before the eyes and ears of the world?

DANDER. Not the people.

HÁJEK. You absolve the people?

DANDER. They don't need absolution they need —

HÁJEK. Yes yes yes they need liberation. One's acutely aware of
it Horatio. But bear with me. (*He gets the cork out with a loud
pop.*) You know our trials old man. You see yourself making
one of those brilliant rhetorical statements from the dock.
Don't you? The kind that move the world. Bring students and
other unstable elements onto the streets. Cause the burning of
an embassy or two and in general leave an omelette flambée on
the faces of your erstwhile hosts. Yes? Something on the lines
of Castro's 'History will absolve me' in reverse, yes?

DANDER. Exactly.

HÁJEK. I thought so. Which might force us to check you — no

pun intended — by turning Klumm into a national hero overnight. (*Tastes the wine.*) Then you'd really be in the shit.

DANDER. A hero out of an ex-Nazi?

HÁJEK. Ah. But you see he never was a Nazi.

DANDER. He was in the Gestapo.

HÁJEK. Horatio. You killed the insect without knowing the full story. I shall be absolutely frank with you. Klumm was volksdeutsch. A German born and bred in the Sudetenland. (*Eating.*) He joined the Czech resistance and his work with our people took him into the Gestapo. In April forty-five an officer in the Gestapo — one Heini Dindl — was in the act of thieving a Corot sketch, six Van Gogh drawings, an early Picasso, two Modiglianis and a Renoir. Millions of dollars' worth of art, my dear — the property of the Republic of Czechoslovakia. (*Chewing.*) Well. The dreadful Dindl — I'm so sorry Horatio — hot-footed it to Buenos Aires with the lot. Yes caro. Your daddy. With our zealous Klumm grimly on his tail. (*Pause.*) Klumm bungled it — which was molto tragico. Because you see there's the little matter of the money Dindl got for those paintings of ours. In Buenos Aires, compañero. (*Pause.*) It's never been recovered. And some who shall be nameless have been in a frightful tizz about it ever since. (*Pause.*) I wonder what your father did with our two million bucks in Japan? Could Heini be the demonic force behind the yen?

DANDER. The Czech people are cowering in servitude and all you can think of is my father's money?

HÁJEK. I do think he's quite sweet, don't you Jana? But that nanny of his — what the devil was her name again?

DANDER. Miss Harriet Stark and I'll thank you to lay off nanny. Her dying words to me were: go out into the world Horatio and be the torch of truth, the flame of conscience.

HÁJEK. Quite. A snobbish English working-class conservative right down to her toenails. Wouldn't she turn in her grave if she knew you'd turned into an armchair revolutionary and a sort of accidental murderer to boot? Come come, coochie. Have a morsel of this divine cheese and pull yourself together. It's fresh from the country. My friend and I have a little shack down there among the comrade peasants. Used to belong to Klinka's chauffeur, as a matter of fact.

DANDER. Is Klinka in on all this.

HÁJEK. Goodness me no. Klinka wouldn't sully his hands with
affairs of state. He's an artist pure and simple, at least in his
own eyes (*Sips wine.*) No no no. The only problem we have
just now with Jiří is his tiresome urge to make a sort of Czech
One Flew Over the Cuckoo's Nest. Can you imagine? (*Sips.*)
Still. I think we've drawn him off the scent with Turp for the
time being.

DANDER. He's hardly a raving dissident, more's the pity.

HÁJEK. I'll give you that. Did you see a film of his called *Fiasco*?
I will say he's the only man I know who labels his goods with
an accurate discription of the contents. Watch him, Horatio.
He'll have no scruples about playing fast and loose with that
unresolved Oedipus complex of yours. *Not* that we take the
unconscious mind very seriously over here. We find it wreaks
havoc with the notion of responsibility. Let any Czech run
away with the idea he has an unconscious mind, we'll be back
to Schweik before you can say there's a spectre haunting Eastern
Europe. (*Lights a thin cheroot.*) Apropos which, this tutor of
yours at Oxford seems to have led you up the odd cul-de-sac
dear boy. Fled the old country in sixty-eight, did he?

DANDER. As if you didn't know.

HÁJEK. I'm not reproaching anybody. I'm class of sixty-eight
myself. Only I went to Cambridge. There's nothing like a
rigorous acquaintance with linguistic philosophy for
straightening out a few of the dialectical wrinkles. Moore,
Wittgenstein, Russell. Ryle and Strawson. (*Grins.*) The
twinkling A.J. Ayer? Young Stoppard must be laughing all the
way to the bank — all those hilarious old philosophical jokes
ringing the till for him every night. Confess. I'll bet the rest of
you scribblers are green with envy. Can there be a dramatist in
England who wouldn't sigh with relief if young Stoppers
vanished in a puff of smoke? (*Sips.*) He must be a tyro's
nightmare, at any rate.

DANDER. If I weren't a tyro, Turp wouldn't have hired me.

HÁJEK. Our garbage department tells me Turp hasn't even a
decent commercial to call his own.

DANDER. Your garbage department! Your spies! Shooting
Klumm will haunt me for the rest of my life.

HÁJEK. What I ask myself is, Horatio: why come here to be
demoralised when you could do it in relative comfort back in
England? (*Icily.*) My information is that Dindl sold the pictures

in Buenos Aires and bought Klumm off with half the proceeds. Klumm squandered his share in the States and went back to Argentina. He arranged your mother's death in a carefully staged accident just after you were born. Then he told your father the same would happen to you unless he turned over his own share of the money. Dindl sent you to England — and promptly vanished.

DANDER. I thought you said Klumm bungled it?

HÁJEK. Oh Jesus, Horatio — the money! How else would you describe Klumm's failure to lay his paws on the gold, old son? (*Smiling.*) Aren't I the clever one? I fix Klinka's rotten old co-production. Klinka gets Turp. Turp gets you. (*Purring.*) And now I've got you, haven't I? Half the population of my department wishes it had you. You wouldn't believe the pushing and shoving that's going on. It's as if they've all begun to believe in Santa Claus again. (*Pause.*) But it's my operation —

DANDER (*making for the door*). Since you won't arrest me — just try and stop me getting out tomorrow.

HÁJEK. Believe me, Horrors. When I close the airports and the frontiers — a flea couldn't get out. (*Crossing to* DANDER.) Exactly where in Japan is Heini Dindl?

DANDER. I've no idea.

HÁJEK. What about those lawyers in Tokyo? (*Smiling, he looks at* JANA.)

DANDER. They're inscrutable.

HÁJEK. Then we shall have to ruminate. You may toddle off for the moment Horatio. Only bear in mind. We have a gun with your prints. We have Klumm's body. One tactless move on your part and the British Embassy'll find you dead on their doorstep. Shot whilst trying to escape after the murder of a Czech national. (*Smiling.*) They won't want to know, dear heart.

DANDER *stands paralysed between apoplexy and despair.*

DANDER (*to* JANA). Are you happy in your work?

JANA. It's what seems to keep everybody happy, Misha.

DANDER *goes.* HÁJEK *fills two glasses and gives one to* JANA. *They touch rims.*

HÁJEK. Na zdraví!

JANA. Na zdraví!

HÁJEK *takes* DANDER'S *gun and points it at* JANA, *firing three shots. They are blanks.* HÁJEK *and* JANA *fall on each other's shoulders, shrieking with laughter.*
Fade out.

Scene Four

The Charles Bridge over the River Vltava. Late the same night.
    KLINKA *stands on the bridge parapet clinging precariously to one of the statues.* DANDER *comes shuffling along, hands in pockets, mildly drunk.* KLINKA *peers down.*

KLINKA. Is it young Dander?

DANDER. I'm drunk.

KLINKA. So am I.

DANDER. What are you doing up there?

KLINKA. Contemplating suicide.

DANDER. Why tonight especially?

KLINKA. Nothing special. I try two or three times a week.

DANDER. What's stopping you?

KLINKA. The secret police won't let me.

    Pause.

DANDER. Why don't you just jump?

KLINKA. There's two of them down there in a patrol boat with machine pistols. If I jump, they'll shoot me.

    Pause.

DANDER. There's a flaw in that somewhere, Jirka.

    KLINKA *lowers himself puffing, to sit on the parapet with his legs dangling.*

KLINKA. Don't you think our species is little more than a vast, evolutionary blunder? Don't you my boy? Looking into your beautiful blue eyes —

DANDER. Don't you mean revolutionary blunder? I mean, if Lenin —

KLINKA. Horatio —

DANDER. Yes?

KLINKA. I shall either get very angry, or burst into tears — if you go on reminding me of the young Klinka who used to stroll up and down this very bridge with his comrades in the thirties. Poor. Innocent. Each and everyone of us with the bit of the October Revolution clenched firmly between his teeth. (*Pause.*) I asked Turp for a screenwriter. Why does he have to send me a cross between a nun and Che Guevara?

DANDER. 'When if not now and who if not I?'

KLINKA. You fell for that one too, did you? (*Looks down over the bridge.*) They've gone. I'm really off this time —

He starts hauling himself to his feet, clutching at the statue. DANDER flings his arms round one of KLINKA'S legs.

KLINKA. Will you please to unleg me Horatio?

DANDER. Don't do it. Come down and we'll go and get really pissed. Just you and me.

KLINKA. No!

Two POLICEMEN with machine pistols stroll across the bridge. They stop and stare at KLINKA, trying to free himself from DANDER'S arms. When KLINKA sees them he subsides from the vertical to a seated position once more. The POLICEMEN go.

KLINKA. Now do you believe me? About *them.*

DANDER. Why don't they want you to kill yourself?

KLINKA. Even you ought to know they've never been keen on the free vote.

DANDER. And they keep you under surveillance all the time?

KLINKA. It's a national sport.

DANDER. I'll bet the people don't approve.

KLINKA. 'The people'? Oh Dander. You're a political dunce aren't you? What am I going to do with you? Funny how abstraction — which I'd thought of its very nature is intangible — can clog the human brain.

DANDER. I'd have thought if you knocked yourself off you'd be doing their job for them.

KLINKA. You are wonderful. Listen. I've followed every twist and turn of the party line for forty years like a tart in thrall to a pimp. You think it was because I was fooled? Not for a minute. All I ever wanted to do was stay alive and make films. I've raised corruption to a high art, Horatio. I'm one of the few people they'd have to account for if I don't die peacefully in my bed. Practically an official hero, in a way. My dear fellow, they only drive honest people to suicide in this country.

DANDER. But you make such awful films —

KLINKA *springs onto the pavement with sudden agility and rounds on* DANDER, *glaring.*

KLINKA (*shouting*). I have made what films I have been allowed to make!

DANDER. I'm sorry.

KLINKA. Gott sei Dank you are to London in the morning or I'd push you off this bridge. Then I'd bring Gustav Turp here and push *him* off. Then I'd bring —

DANDER. Jirka I think I'm the innocent victim at the centre of a conspiracy —

KLINKA. You are, huh? It's probably the only time you'll ever command serious attention in your life then. (*Going.*) I wish to know nothing.

DANDER. I'm in a real fix, Jirka. And I just thought you might —

KLINKA (*still going*). I just definitely wish to know nothing.

DANDER. Did you ever?

KLINKA (*goes, shouting*). Never!

DANDER *stands looking after* KLINKA *mournfully. Then he slowly climbs up on the parapet and jumps off. There is a loud splash.*
Fade out.

Scene Five

A small beergarden near Prague Airport the following morning. Sunshine. Faint brass band music. The occasional whine of a passing jet.
      KLINKA *and* JANA *sit with glasses of beer. On the table there is also an elegant white box tied with green ribbon.*

JANA (*tapping the box*). What's this?

KLINKA. Cakes for Ludmila. (*Looks at his watch.*) Where is the boy? I thought you said the hospital discharged him early this morning?

JANA. So they did. And I sent a car to his hotel to fetch him here. (*Pause.*) He's fine. He landed in one metre of water and three metres of mud.

A jet whines softly, high up.

KLINKA (*looks up*). That could be Turp's plane. I've a feeling I'm doomed this time. (*Pause.*) Why didn't I quit in sixty-eight like everybody else?

JANA. They had something to live for, didn't they?

KLINKA. You know. My grandmother had a conviction that one day General Eisenhower would liberate Prague on a white horse. Do you think if he had you'd have been born human?

JANA. Well. You have Ludmila.

KLINKA. You think I stayed here to keep that bitch out of the calaboose? (*Squashes the box of cakes with his fist.*) If she could get into bed with your Comrade Hájek she'd have a passport to Los Angeles before you could say flower-power. (*Wistfully.*) Come to think of it, sixty-eight saw the withering of flower-power as well. Who says capitalism doesn't have its moments of poetry and sadness too?

A WAITER *brings a telephone to* JANA *and whispers in her ear, holding out the receiver.*

KLINKA. Who's this?

JANA. Horatio's agent. A Mr Bunce.

KLINKA. I'll take it — (*Grabbing the phone.*) Bunce? Klinka here. Dander's coming right back on the next plane. What? (*Pause.*) Yes *Dander.* (*Pause.*) Bunce you are through to a beergarden on the road to Prague Airport. (*Pause.*) This is not the Beverly Wilshire Los Angeles, no sir. (*Pause.*) Will you shut up and listen? (*Pause.*) Why shouldn't I talk to you like that? Everybody talks to me like that. (*Pause.*) It's nothing to do with totalitarianism, you fool. Is your rambling connected with social democracy? (DANDER *enters, pale and snuffling with a bad cold.*) Listen Bunce. All I want to ask is why you sent me this teddy-tales merchant. What? (*Pause.*) No, I'd say the boy's a kind of ideological Pinocchio. Last night he fell in the Vltava. (*Pause.*) No I am not chewing the phone Bunce. Vltava is the name of a very beautiful river we have here. (*Pause.*) Yes. And

promise me you'll go and shit in your own sombrero as well?
(*Pause.*) Good. Right. (*Slams down* the phone, regards DANDER
with compassion.) You ever tried the William Morris agency
Horatio?

DANDER. I could never desert Natty. (*Sneezes.*) Not the man
who took me on after reading my first play.

KLINKA. What was that? 'Flopsy, Mopsy, Cotton-tail and
Trotsky'?

DANDER (*firmly*). 'A Small Person's Guide to the Bourgeoisie'.

KLINKA. If he took you on he must have a private income.

DANDER. He has a lot of ostrich feathers in a warehouse in
Pretoria.

KLINKA. Why is he convinced you're some genius called
McPherson? Says he spoke to McPherson in Sofia last night
and he's radioed Turp's plane this morning confirming Gus
has definitely not been lumbered with Dander.

DANDER. Oh dear. And on top, I think I've got pneumonia.
(*Beadily.*) At least we now know why you picked that spot for
your pseudo-suicides. Just in case you fell off by accident!

KLINKA. Who's this McPherson dammit? Should I know? Royal
Court? National? Royal Shakespeare Company? Has he any
screen credits? Don't by coy, Horatio. What did he do — win
the Golden Mouse at the Bangkok Film Festival?

DANDER. We were at Oxford together. He wrote a fringe rock
musical on the life of Savonarola, amongst other things.

KLINKA. One thing in Bunce's favour. The way things are going,
he must hate Turp.

DANDER. The consensus among Natty's authors is that there's
something profoundly amiss with the psychodynamics of his
unconscious mind. I do appreciate that hardly squares with
your more Pavlovian view over here, but —

KLINKA. What hardly squares? We have sixty crypto-analysts
serving beer and mending punctures in Prague alone. Your car
breaks down in Bratislava? The mechanic'll have you in
transference while he's overhauling the gearbox.

DANDER. According to a very wicked person I met called
Hájek —

KLINKA (*to* JANA). He's met Hájek? Didn't I ask you to take
care of him? To cradle him in your bosom till he sprouts

wings and flies back to kiddievision this afternoon?

DANDER. Jirka, she's involved in the conspiracy.

KLINKA. Do enlighten me. She's involved in so many.

DANDER. I tried to tell you when we were on the Charles Bridge last night.

KLINKA. Horatio. Last night my wife was in bed with some damned Russian or other and I was feeling quite impervious to lesser egos.

DANDER. Yesterday evening. In this creature's flat. I was manoeuvred into shooting to death a man called Klumm. What do you make of that, since you appear to know the ropes so well they haven't choked you yet?

KLINKA. Jaroslav Klumm?

DANDER. You knew him?

KLINKA (*laughing*). The wedding photographer and part-time clown? Oh Dander!

DANDER. Well I for one don't think it's very funny to take the life of another human being.

KLINKA. Klumm isn't human — he's East German.

DANDER. Was. And I'll thank you not to lay the iniquities of Klumm at the door of the entire German nation.

KLINKA. He was little more than a faltering life-support system in search of a brain. (*Drinks.*) You'll have to do better than that if you want to bring down Stalinism single-handed my boy.

DANDER. I certainly hope that for once you don't know the half of it. Between them, Jana and Hájek have got me in what nanny used to call a web of intrigue. You think you're getting rid of me? I'm technically a murderer and those two are using it to blackmail me.

KLINKA. I'm deeply ashamed of you Jana.

JANA (*to* DANDER). One of Pan Klinka's many heresies Misha, is a failure to grasp the logic of historical necessity. It makes him lovable but unreliable. (*Sternly.*) You'll say no more about these matters which are confidential to the State.

KLINKA. No my darling. *You* will get on the phone to Hájek and tell him my friend Dander leaves safe and sound in that plane or I shall personally lie down under its bloody wheels!

JANA (*rising*). Don't be ridiculous Jirka. You and I are due at the airport to meet Mr Turp Come. Milos is waiting. (*Going.*) I think you'll find Misha is rooted to the spot. (*Goes.*)

KLINKA. Got you across a barrel, have they?

DANDER (*primly*). I don't wish to embroil you any further Jirka.

KLINKA. You're a prim little bugger, you know.

DANDER. I know. Even a certain Miss Harriet Stark was impressed by her own handiwork. And you're a braggart amongst all the other worrying things you are. Lie down under the plane wheels indeed! It's a bit late in the day to start talking to *these* people like a hysterical suffragette.

KLINKA. What on earth prompted you to jump off that bridge?

DANDER. I wanted to be a big fish in a small river! (*Rises, shaking and sneezing.*) The sort of person you are — I reckon even if you did stick your neck out a millimetre the Kremlin'd hang a large medal round it.

KLINKA. Oh Dander —

DANDER. What?

TOGETHER. Looking into your beautiful blue eyes —

They both laugh. KLINKA *turns and walks away a little to stand with his back to* DANDER, *looking out at the countryside.*

KLINKA. When I was a boy I used to cycle out into this countryside on summer days. (*Pause.*) Used to sit in the grass and dream of becoming a sort of Czech Jean Renoir. (*Pause.*) Used to sit there all day, reading Kleist . . . Büchner . . . Strindberg . . . Hauptmann —

DANDER. Yes? When decent communists were being tortured and persecuted in Germany and Austria? Not to mention those dying in Spain —

Pause.

KLINKA (*turning*). What could you do to my conscience Horatio, that the ghosts of all those fallen comrades can't? Not to mention the victims of our own people. (*Pause.*) History is the midwife of revolution? It isn't, Horatio. It's an old woman in a back street with a dirty knitting needle.

DANDER. Nobody's irredeemable —

KLINKA *smiles. He crosses to* DANDER *and embraces him in a bear-hug.*
KLINKA *steps back a little, holding* DANDER'S *shoulders. He wags a gently reproachful finger under* DANDER'S *nose.*

KLINKA. You are a menace, dear boy. You are a menace.

He kisses DANDER *firmly on both cheeks and goes.* DANDER *sits. Behind him, a* WAITER *clears a table.*
LUDMILA KLINKOVÁ *enters: a beautiful, sad-looking woman in her late thirties. She wears a summer dress, a wide-brimmed hat and sunglasses. She stands lighting a cigarette and speaks to the* WAITER, *ordering champagne in Czech. He goes.*

LUDMILA. Mr Dander?

DANDER (*turning*). Yes?

LUDMILA. Ludmila Klinková. How do you do?

DANDER (*rising*). How do you do? I'm afraid your husband's just left. He's gone to the airport for Gustav Turp.

LUDMILA. I know. I've just seen Jirka. (*Sitting.*) He told me to buy you a drink and look after you.

DANDER. He has a habit of doing that. And you should see what happens —

LUDMILA. Believe me, I do know. We had a row this morning about you. About him throwing you off the film.

DANDER. Well. I don't think I measure up to his obviously very high standards.

LUDMILA. Rubbish.

DANDER. I beg your pardon?

LUDMILA. Klinka has no standards. He's a buffoon.

Pause.

DANDER. I'm sorry things are going badly between you and him.

LUDMILA. You mustn't confuse impertinence with a relaxed social manner Mr Dander. No. Don't apologise. It's Jirka. He seems to quit people in all sorts of unlikely places, leaving them — well how shall I put it in your case? Bereft of your impeccably good English manners?

DANDER. Manners? The redundant mask of an exhausted class? (*Pause.*) Though mind you, I sometimes pine for the archaic values myself.

LUDMILA. You find me archaic? I look and sound archaic to the little grocer?

DANDER (*as the* WAITER *enters with champagne*). You look fantastic.

LUDMILA. Thank you. Join me in a glass of cold champagne. (*The* WAITER *opens the wine with a flourish, and pours.*) I take it you've read a literal translation of Jirka's script?

DANDER. Er — yes.

LUDMILA. That's just how I feel about it. (*Drinks.*) You realise of course, that every Czech who *was* anyone — is in London, Paris, Rome or New York. (*Pause.*) All except Ludmila Klinková.

DANDER. Don't you think that might have been part of the trouble in the first place?

LUDMILA. Trouble? What trouble?

DANDER. The embourgeoisification of the revolutionary intelligentsia?

LUDMILA. Mr Dander —

DANDER. Yes?

LUDMILA. Are you a fucking red?

DANDER. I'm beginning to think I'm a political orphan. Not to mention being one in real life, so to speak.

LUDMILA. This entire country is an orphan you farouche boy. Orphaned by history. Lock stock and revolution that you're clearly so fond of.

DANDER. What's more, it seems my father may have been an art thief.

LUDMILA. It's the best kind of investment there is.

DANDER. A Nazi art thief.

LUDMILA (*yawning*). You do rather have a run-of-the-mill life story don't you?

DANDER *is duly abashed and hunches over his champagne.*

DANDER. I suppose you've starred in a lot of Mr Klinka's films —

LUDMILA. One doesn't 'star' in a Klinka. One merely adds tone to an otherwise vulgar pastiche of his latest cinematic idol.

DANDER. Who's that at the moment?

LUDMILA. Fassbinder.

DANDER. Has Jirka directed a lot of films here?

LUDMILA. Over the centuries, a Cocteau or two. A Carol Reed. Three Hitchcocks, a Godard, a Truffaut, a Chabrol and a mini-Visconti. (*Sips.*) As you can see, I've had to be versatile.

DANDER. You strike me as a deeply wounded lady Mrs Klinkova. May I touch your hand?

LUDMILA. You may.

She extends a fine thin brown hand. DANDER *reverently touches it. He takes it gently in his own.*

DANDER. You must be very famous over here.

LUDMILA (*snatching her hand away*). Dander we are all perfectly well aware that to be famous anywhere between East Berlin and Vladivostock rates about as much distinction as a bit part in a Hindu musical. However. Should you remain in our glorious republic much longer —

DANDER. Yes?

LUDMILA. And have the privilege of meeting any other distinguished actresses —

DANDER. Yes?

LUDMILA. I wouldn't refer to them as being famous 'over here' or they'll box your ears.

Pause.

DANDER. I've learned more in the last twenty-four hours than in the whole of my twenty-five years Mrs Klinkova. (*Pause.*) Thank you.

LUDMILA (*tenderly*). The whole of his twenty-five years! Horatio, I feel a whim coming over me. I think I shall take you with me to the film festival at Karlovy Vary. There I am someone.There I am important. Why don't you stay, and to hell with Klinka?

DANDER. Well. (*Pause.*) A Mr Hájek I met made a very similar suggestion.

LUDMILA. You know Hájek?

DANDER. We've passed the time of day. I don't think you'd like him. He's something in the secret police.

LUDMILA. Darling. I think in you — destiny has forged a link
between me and Hollywood. You may kiss my cheek if you
wish —

> DANDER *moves round the table eagerly to do so.* KLINKA
> *enters with* GUSTAV TURP *and* JANA. TURP *is a small
> pugnacious man with small eyes gone rheumy with the effort
> of trying to twinkle. He is festooned with plastic bags
> containing various duty-free items.*
> *All three stand watching as* LUDMILA *leans back with eyes
> closed to receive* DANDER'S *kiss.*

TURP. McPherson! (DANDER *springs back.*) Get off that judy
and take some of these duty-frees will you? (*As* DANDER
does so.) Jeery you never told me what a honey! (*Descends on*
LUDMILA, *seizes her hand and kisses it.*) Madam may I say
how lovely you are? (*Turning.*) Jeery, you old dog!

KLINKA. My name pronounces Jiří, Gus. Please. Jiří.

> TURP *grabs one of the bags from* DANDER, *takes out a large
> box of perfume. Presses it into* LUDMILA'S *hands.*

DANDER. Excuse me Mr Turp —

TURP. What now? You want a kiss from me as well, you lousy
impostor?

DANDER. It's true I'm not McPherson, but —

TURP. Don't you tell me who you are. It's true you're not
Dander. I had a message from that screwy agent of yours. He
sent Dander to Los Angeles, poor kid. Bunce radioed my
plane he spoke to you on the phone in Warsaw last night, Mac.
You in person. (*He stamps his foot.*) So what's this we're now
standing on? Pasadena?

DANDER. Czechoslovakia.

TURP. Right. So you wish to remain incognito? It's okay by me.
(*Grinning at* KLINKA.) Who's this he writes a musical about?
Sarovanola? What is it, a suburb in Naples? (*To* DANDER.)
Sounds to me like something you sit a monkey on and play in
the street. (*Crossing to gloat over* LUDMILA.) With Jeery's
talent and you in the star role Mrs K. — it's going to be a
smasheroo.

DANDER. I'm Dander, I tell you. Wasn't it me you wanted?

TURP. How the hell do I know what I want till I see who I get?
Now shut up will you? Little screenwriters should be seen and

not heard. I'll deal with you later. (*To* LUDMILA.) Champers, is it? (*To* JANA, *snapping his fingers.*) Champers all round in whatever's Polish for be bloody quick about it. Eh sweetheart? (JANA *goes and* TURP *subsides onto a chair wheezing.*) I have to tell you this Mrs K. and I really mean it. Jeery's heard some things about me. Well it's all true. I'm nothing but a cheap stereotype climbed life's great barbed wire fence on the necks of the guys underneath.

LUDMILA. Really? Then you'll soon find yourself among friends over here Mr Turp.

TURP. Great! (*Lighting a cigar.*) So I'll throw it to you without any frills. The Turp stereo is, you might say — unique. What's going to get to you Mrs K. is the sheer scale of my achievement in this area. I mean that. Old Gus is going to get this film made, I don't care whose balls I have to chew over there in the Kremlin.

LUDMILA. I'd thought your kind of stereotype went out when I was a little girl. I'm so relieved.

TURP *throws his head back laughing, coughing, braying, slapping his knee with his flat palm.* JANA *enters with a* WAITER *who proceeds to serve champagne.*

TURP (*hooting and clutching his heart*). Don't do it Mrs K. Don't kill me —

LUDMILA. I certainly don't wish to overload your pacemaker.

TURP (*in paroxysms of delight*). How did she know, Jeery? What a princess!

LUDMILA (*lighting a cigarette*). Jirka darling. He's such a *grotesque* little wanker.

There is a silence. TURP *is stunned, then meanly transformed.*

TURP. Lady. I've got two million dollars lined up and half the Polish film bureaucracy in my pocket.

LUDMILA. It will be of no avail to you here in Prague, Mr Turp.

TURP (*subsiding with an effort*). Come come Mrs K. Give a little take a little. That's what I mean, for Christ's sake. In Prague. We got to learn to love each other — all righty?

Whilst TURP *is speaking,* KLUMM — *dressed as a* WAITER — *is crossing the stage with a tray of beers, unseen by all except* DANDER. *Ashen,* DANDER *struggles to rise. With a hideous wink at* JANA, KLUMM *goes.*

TURP. McPherson. Tell this lady who I am, will you?

DANDER (*croaking*). Tyrannosaurus Rex?

TURP (*shouting*). You're fired! (DANDER *faints to the ground*).

KLINKA *kneels beside* DANDER, *trying to hold him in his arms.* TURP *wanders over chewing his cigar, morbidly if remotely fascinated.* KLINKA *supports* DANDER *with one arm and lightly pats his cheek.*

KLINKA. Horatio? (*Pause.*) Horatio?

TURP. First time I've known anybody take it quite so hard.

KLINKA. The boy is not well. He tried to commit suicide last night —

TURP. On *my* film?

KLINKA. My film.

TURP. He's my writer. Who just fired him?

KLINKA. I already fired him yesterday. (*He has his hands under* DANDER'S *armpits, straining to lift him onto a chair.*)

TURP. On whose say-so? What the hell are you trying to do to me Klinka?

LUDMILA *is powdering her face. She snaps the compact shut, rising. As she goes, with a cool smile at* TURP.

LUDMILA. At a rough guess, Mr Turp — I'd say he's trying to get your dander up. (*Goes.*)

KLINKA *is struggling to get* DANDER *onto a chair. He finally makes it with* JANA'S *help, whilst* TURP *stands in front of him haranguing.*

TURP. You know what I've done for you Jeery? Last night I wired Redford, Newman, Harris, de Niro. I got a call booked through to James Caan this afternoon. You want a co-production or don't you? You think I'm not sticking my neck out on this deal? You think I fly to Warsaw every day of my life? (*Kicks* DANDER'S *foot.*) Ah come on, Jeery. These fringe kids are ten a penny. How about a cable to Sozhenitskyn?

KLINKA (*rounds on* TURP *shouting*). Jana will you get this bacterium out of my sight?

TURP. Right. Fine (*Pause.*) Right right. Fine fine. (*Pause.*) Great. Terrific. (*To* JANA.) My duty-frees, if you don't mind —

JANA *gathers up his plastic bags.* KLINKA *is feeling* DANDER'S *pulse.* TURP *goes to* KLINKA *and slaps* DANDER'S *arm down.*

TURP. He'll live, Jeery. Will you? I mean. When in the last twenty years did you give us a 'Jaws'? A 'Close Encounters'? (*Pats* KLINKA'S *cheek.*) I really mean that. (*Grins.*) You need me. You're on the brink, sweetheart. With my contacts in your film export department I can have you tarred and feathered and thrown into the goddamn Danube!

He goes, trying to register truculent hauteur. JANA *is following with the plastic bags when* DANDER *sits bolt upright.*

DANDER. Klumm's alive!

JANA. I wish he were Misha. For your sake. (*Going.*) You will both wait here, please? I must have directions from Comrade Hájek. (*Goes.*)

DANDER. You didn't see Klumm, Jirka? Dressed as a waiter?

KLINKA. Delusions, Horatio. (*Pours a glass of champagne.*) Here. Drink this. You are ill, and frightened. It will make you feel better.

DANDER (*sipping*). Frightened?

KLINKA. I hope you are wise enough to be scared shitless. (*Pause.*) I squeezed a little of your story out of her.

DANDER. How?

KLINKA (*grinning*). It is only five minutes to the airport. But long enough for Miloš to explain to her in what fashion some friends of his could break her bones. (*Pause.*) I am sorry what you learned about your father. But Hájek doesn't want him for his war-crimes Horatio. Only for the money. He is quite happy that you shot Klumm. Klumm worked for a rival of Hájek's in the secret police called Krk. Comrade Krk. These men and at least one other faction will do anything to get to Heini Dindl. Looking into your beautiful blue eyes, my boy — you are the most desirable hostage in town.

DANDER. I could swear I saw Klumm.

KLINKA. Every night of my life, I see Jan Masaryk falling from a balcony of the foreign ministry in Prague. (*Pause.*) It wonderfully concentrates my will to live, Horatio.

DANDER. You and Miloš threatened to *torture* Jana?

KLINKA. Unpardonable, wasn't it? And all on account of you. If it's any consolation, it also means I have broken Klinka's First Law: Jiří über alles. (*Taking a newspaper from his pocket.*) There's also a little item I noticed in gruesome Gus's London Evening News on the way here from Ruzyně. Just a few lines at the bottom of a page somewhere. (*Finding the page and reading out:*) 'German recluse disappears from mountain retreat in Northern Japan, after a fracas involving two agents of an unidentified foreign power. The two men — said to be suffering fractures and severe contusions from karate blows — were bustled on stretchers from the scene in a black van with false registration plates.' How's that for a wheeze Liebling? To my mind it rings a little bell that chimes Há-jek, Há-jek —

JANA *enters.*

JANA. I have instructions from Comrade Hájek, Misha. You will return to Prague. You will meet him in the small park opposite your hotel at two pm. this afternoon. (*Turning to* KLINKA.) Comrade Klinka. You have a choice between immediate house arrest or making up your quarrel with Turp and getting him to Karlovy Vary for the duration of the film festival. (*Smiling tartly.*) I'm sure Ludmila will be happy to drive you. She's going.

KLINKA. Oh will she? And why won't Miloš drive us?

JANA. Guess.

KLINKA. He's had one our famous State coronaries?

JANA. Right! (*To* DANDER.) Hájek says to remind you the Heini Dindl file is still open. Furthermore, Operation Codename Dindl Swindle is now your baby Misha. (*Menacingly.*) Or else.

DANDER. Or else what?

JANA. Or you'll end up in the river again. And this time Hájek won't have you dredged out. (*Goes.*)

DANDER. My baby? I wish I knew whose baby *I* am. (*He bares his forearm.*) I can't believe it. Nazi Dindl blood flowing through those veins? I'd hoped he was a transistor tycoon or something over there in Japan. You know? Just a straight-forward chap who couldn't face the responsibility of guiding little Horatio through life's tortuous labyrinth. (*Pause.*) Take me to your father? (*Pause.*) None of it sinks in, somehow.

KLINKA. It had better, Horatio. And you'd better keep that rendezvous with Hájek or you'll do your sinking in the Vltava. You heard what she said about Miloš? I'm off to lick Turp's boots. You betcha!

DANDER. I'm damned if I'm going to lick Hájek's!

KLINKA. What's it to you? If your father was a Nazi you hate him — no? They want his two million bucks? You scratch Hájek's back, he might throw you out of Czechoslovakia in one whole piece. (*Gently.*) What does it feel like young Danderle? To be on the spot where some of us have been warming our backsides for thirty years?

DANDER (*shouting*). Turncoat!

KLINKA. What else? If I didn't turn I'd freeze. Just a threadbare old bastard down on his luck as usual. (*Thumps* DANDER'S *back.*) Bear up, my boy. (*Going.*) I'll have the patron send you a stiff drink and a sandwich, eh? And what about a nice record? A little music, it always helps when coming to terms. (*Goes.*)

DANDER *sags miserably onto a chair, sneezing. After a moment a* WAITER *brings out a large whisky and a sandwich.* DANDER *sips at the drink. The beergarden loudspeakers begin to play 'Whose Baby Now?'.* Fade out.

Act Two

Scene One

A small park in central Prague. Afternoon the same day. Sunshine. Faint crackly music (Smetana's The Bartered Bride*) from loudspeakers on distant lamp posts.*

A park bench. Behind it, seated on rickety wooden chairs tipped against a long green fence, are HÁJEK'S two HEAVIES. Each wears dark glasses and is pretending to read the Czech newspaper Rudé Právo.

A thin serious-looking YOUNG MAN is establishing himself on the bench. He wears a carefully ironed beige shirt, slacks, and sandles over socks. From a briefcase he takes a wurst sandwich, a copy of Rudé Právo and a thermos of coffee. He puts Rudé Právo beside him on the bench. He smooths a paper napkin on his knees and carefully places the sandwich on it. Pours himself a cup of coffee. Sits sipping the coffee and staring straight ahead through steel-rimmed glasses. He nibbles the sandwich.

DANDER — with his jacket slung over his shoulder — comes along hobbling slightly. After a moment of hesitation he sits beside the YOUNG MAN, with Rudé Právo between them.

A silence. The YOUNG MAN nibbles nervously. DANDER is looking at him sideways.

DANDER. Excuse me. I suppose you don't, er — speak English?

The YOUNG MAN stiffly ignores him throughout the whole encounter. DANDER imitates a speaking mouth with his hand.

DANDER. Anglicky?

The HEAVIES are peeping. The YOUNG MAN gulps nervously. DANDER turns to look at the HEAVIES. Their newspapers hide their faces.

DANDER *(to YOUNG MAN)*. Turd face? *(Pause.)* Prick nose? *(Pause.)* Whore's son of a Chilean fascist's donkey? *(Relaxes.)*

So glad you're not deceitful. Like some I've met lately.
(Pause.) Must be hell in these little countries language-wise.
I mean. We don't quite see Czech becoming the lingua franca
of the United Nations. Do we?

There is a sudden loud burst of The Bartered Bride, *which*
crackles away to silence.

DANDER. Good old Smetana! (YOUNG MAN *sniffs.*) May I?
(Picks up Rudé Právo.) Rudé Právo. *(Pause.)* Red Truth? *(Pause.)*
Frankly it's my personal experience that that statement is
often a contradiction in terms. *(Pause.)* Naturally one knows
the official side of things over here's nothing but lies. But
deceit for purely personal advantage, now. Well it seems to
have caught the imagination of every single person I've met so
far. *(Pause.)* This demoralises, in my opinion. *(Pause.)* Of course
now, if you could understand me you'd say capitalism's all
lies too. And you'd be right. *(Pause.)* There's a very subtle
moral line through all this I'm sure. If only I could tease it out
from the surrounding confusion. *(Leans back with an amiable*
expression.) Could the venerable Trotsky himself have teased
it out?

At the word 'Trotsky' the HEAVIES *lower their papers. The*
YOUNG MAN *deftly twitches back his paper from* DANDER'S
knees. DANDER *stamps his foot.*

DANDER. I think there's a little stone in there, you know. *(To his*
foot:) A dear little chunk of Czechoslovakian gravel.

He bends to slip off his shoe. Feels for the stone. Kneads his
foot dreamily. The HEAVIES *silently spring forward. They*
whip the YOUNG MAN *backwards over the bench, slap*
elastoplast over his mouth, handcuffs on his wrists, and pass
him over the fence where he is hustled away by two MEN.

The HEAVIES *resume their chairs and their papers.* DANDER
straightens up, sees the vacant space — the paper, briefcase and
thermos. He stands up and looks round the park. Sits down
again, staring thoughtfully at his feet.

A plump old PEASANT WOMAN *in a black dress and head-*
square enters pushing a pram. The pram is new and shiny,
with a charming lace extending hood to protect the baby's
face from the sun.

PEASANT. Dobrý den —

DANDER. Dobrý den —

*She sits down heavily, sighing and wheezing, the pram beside
the bench. A rattle hangs from the hood. She flicks it,
clucking and cooing. She takes the Rudé Právo and hands it to*
DANDER.

DANDER. Not mine. (*Loudly.*) Er — not mine.

PEASANT. Prosím?

DANDER (*pointing to himself.*) Anglický. Angličan.

*She shakes her head disapprovingly, takes needles and wool
from the pram and starts knitting.* DANDER *looks at his watch.
Leans back drumming his fingers on his knees. There is another
burst of Smetana, which again dies away in a crackle.*

DANDER. Good old Smetana!

PEASANT. Smetana? Tcha! (*Takes a transistor from the pram and
waves it vigorously.*) Rolling Stons —

She turns it on. Loud rock booms out. DANDER *puts his hands
to his ears. She switches it off huffily and sits clucking and
knitting. Occasionally she looks at* DANDER *with hostility,
but gently falls asleep and begins to snore through his next
speech.*

DANDER. Dear old peasant head. (*Pause.*) Wish I were inside it.
(*Hums a few bars of* The Volga Boatman.) Wish I inhabited
those memories. That's what it's all about. The real people.
The indignant masses. (*Pause.*) I hope your frail boat's come
into harbour, dear old peasant lady. (*Pause.*) Birch forests.
Wheatfields. The endless rolling steppe. (*Fondly.*) Red
cossacks. White nights. Mayakovsky. Mandelstam. Gorky.
(*Pause.*) The ambivalent Yevtushenko —

At this list of names the HEAVIES *lower their papers.*
DANDER *becomes aware he hasn't got rid of the stone. Tries
his foot gingerly on the ground. Bends to remove his shoe and
sock.*
Whilst he is occupied, the HEAVIES *repeat their previous
performance, with the old* PEASANT WOMAN.
When DANDER *looks up the old lady has been spirited away
and the* HEAVIES *are behind their papers. He stands and
stares hard at them. Shrugs, and sits. After a moment he
shuffles along the bench to the pram and flicks the rattle.*

DANDER. Coochie coochie —

Silence. He peers inside the pram. Thrusts his hand in and

brings out a large plucked goose. Sits holding it by the neck wonderingly.
HÁJEK *enters with a jaunty step, debonair in a light summer suit and Chekhovian straw hat.*

HÁJEK. There you are Horatio. What on earth are you doing with that dead bird?

DANDER (*drops it into the pram.*) It seems to have been abandoned by its nanny. I expect she's gone for a pee.

HÁJEK *sits down, crosses his legs elegantly and takes a cigarette from a gold case. A town clock strikes two.*

HÁJEK. How's that for timing? I'm an absolute punctuality freak.

DANDER. D'you think this is a good place to meet, after all?

HÁJEK. Why ever not?

DANDER. I was wondering. (*Turns to look at the* HEAVIES.) I have an uneasy feeling people are being spirited away.

HÁJEK (*glances at the* HEAVIES). What have my gorillas been up to now?

DANDER. So that's it! And if there'd been a baby in that pram instead of a dead goose?

HÁJEK. Well naturally the child would have been arrested too.

DANDER *gapes.* HÁJEK *laughs and pats his knee.*

Dear me, Horatio. Can't you take a joke? No one's been arrested. The boys were ordered to keep you in a sort of . . . quarantine. That's all. They aren't any too bright. Tend to take me a bit literally and so on and so forth.

DANDER. I thought I was going mad.

HÁJEK. Join the club.

DANDER. I even thought I saw Klumm walking about dressed as a waiter. In that beer-garden where Jana so faithfully passed on your plans for us all.

HÁJEK. She told me. You really must try to get a grip on yourself old boy.

DANDER. It's a bit late for that when I'm well and truly in yours.

HÁJEK. You really mustn't rush about Prague jumping off bridges. The river patrol had a ghastly time scraping the mud off you. And what would Miss Harriet Stark have had to say about it?

DANDER. Nanny was a stickler for the large moral gesture.

HÁJEK. Ah me. You're definitely not of this nasty wicked world Horatio. And one doubts if you'll survive long in the west either. (*Sighs.*)

DANDER. I wonder what it is about me?

HÁJEK. Who knows? (*Pause.*) Who knows what strange conjunction there was over there in Buenos Aires long ago. (*Pause.*) A hot tropical night. A sickle moon. Throbbing guitars. Heini Dindl rushing from brothel to brothel with sacks of gold dangling from every button.

DANDER. Brothel to broth —

HÁJEK. Where do you think you were born? In a bloody manger?

DANDER *goes for his throat, but sees the* HEAVIES *lower their papers. He moves back and shuffles away from* HAJEK *to sit miserably hunched whilst* HAJEK *fastidiously straightens his collar and dusts at his suit.*

I thought you were non-violent, Horrors? I thought you'd come here to set us all to rights? (DANDER *sits up straight, folds his arms and crosses his legs, blank-faced.*) That's better. Now listen. I've been doing a lot of homework, some of which arrived in the diplomatic bag from Tokyo this morning. Well. Lovely for him but ghastly for you, Dindl's alive and well. The trouble is he keeps on giving my chaps the slip and now he's disappeared altogether.

DANDER. I disown him. Whatever you want, I won't do it.

HÁJEK (*patiently*). It's a sine qua non of a regime like ours that every one of its hapless citizens would like to get out. Has this dawned yet, Horatio? And little me is no exception. Much as I'd like to assist the population of the entire republic in their honest dreams of a life in the golden west — I've been thinking more of number one lately. (*Smiling.*) I've taken a huge, a simply enormous decision about you Horrors. I'm sending you to Japan. Your daddy's holed up on some Nip mountain or other, and I honestly do think it's time there was a reunion.

DANDER (*rising*). Excuse me —

HÁJEK (*snapping*). No I shan't. I've never considered this job quite my métier from the start. I'm much too fastidious, and

I'm off. You'll do as I say or I shall liquidate you, find Heini, disembowel him out of sheer malice — and forget the whole thing.

DANDER (*going*). I don't see any room in you for moral growth. None at all. (HÁJEK *snaps his fingers, the* HEAVIES *stand up threateningly and* DANDER *freezes.*) Anyway. What makes you think Dindl would cough up to save me? He hasn't exactly had a fixation on me for the last twenty-five years.

HÁJEK. I'll throw in a bonus, Dander. We have lots of friends in BOSS if you'd like Bunce terminated.

We hear the sound of children's voices and a red ball comes bouncing onstage to DANDER'S *feet. He picks it up.*

DANDER. Trotsky once said —

HÁJEK (*snapping irritably*). Trotsky said morality lies outside history, you little prig!

DANDER (*looks at the* HEAVIES, *who are behind their papers again*). When I've restored this ball to its rightful owners, I'm going to give you a piece of my mind. (*Goes off with the ball.*)

HÁJEK (*shaking his fist*). Trotsky indeed!

The gesture has an unfortunate resemblance to the communist clenched fist of solidarity. The HEAVIES *lower their papers and exchange glances. They spring on* HÁJEK, *slap elastoplast across his mouth, handcuffs on his wrists, and whip him over the fence. All three go off, the* HEAVIES *dragging* HÁJEK. *There is the rude blare of a distant diesel train and a sad little spurt of Smetana.* DANDER *returns. He stands looking round for* HÁJEK, *scratching his head.* JANA *enters.*

JANA. You must come with me at once, Misha.

DANDER. You haven't seen Hájek by any chance? (*He crosses to the* HEAVIES' *chairs, gazes down at the copies of Rudé Právo.*)

JANA. There's been a bit of an upheaval in our department. A bit of a lunchtime putsch, to tell you the truth. I'm to take you to the Ministry of the Interior at once.

DANDER. It's funny. One minute he was sitting there quoting Trotsky, and the next he was —

JANA. Quoting who?

DANDER. Oh dear! (*Pause.*) The gorillas?

JANA. Precisely. Oh dear!

DANDER. But it was my fault —

JANA. What isn't? Hájek's thugs aren't renowned for catching the fleeting nuance, you know.

DANDER. Well it serves him right, considering what he was trying to bully me into. (*Staunchly.*) I refuse to mourn.

JANA. Watch out. You're slipping, Misha.

DANDER. Is nobody immune? I'm not crowing, you know.

JANA. Very wise. I wouldn't if I were you. Not before we know who's replaced Hájek. (DANDER *starts wheeling the pram.*) What are you doing with that?

DANDER (*patting the pram*). There's been one of those tiny injustices in this park today that betray the worm at the core of the apple. (*Going with* JANA.) I intend to see a certain little lady gets her dinner back.

Fade out.

Fade in:

Scene Two

A large room at the Ministry of the Interior. COMRADE KRK *sits behind a large desk with a file and a diplomatic bag in front of him. He is a plump greying man in a dark suit, cream shirt, dark red silk tie with a large knot.*

KLÁRA — *a middle-aged woman with close-cropped grey hair — sits to one side of the desk. She wears an austere black costume and a pristine white shirt.*

A long high gauze screen upstage functions as a wall. There is a bust of Lenin on a pedestal, a Czech flag and a Russian flag.

DANDER *enters backwards clutching the goose by the neck.*

KRK. Ah, Mr McPherson. Do sit down.

DANDER (*sitting*). Dander.

KRK. Have you ever seen a diplomatic bag?

KRK *lifts the bag, but* DANDER'S *eyes are on the bird — at which he is plucking wistfully.* DANDER *springs up towards* KLÁRA *with outstretched hand.*

DANDER. Can't say I have. How do you do?

KRK (*pained*). Please, Mr McPherson. No time for frivolity. These are the Tokyo despatches.

DANDER. Has somebody despatched Hájek?

KRK. There's been what I think you'd call a departmental shuffle in this ministry. I am Comrade Krk, whose sad duty it is to wade through the muddle left behind by the Trotskyist and counter-revolutionary Zionist Hájek. (*Pause: presses his finger-tips together.*) The Minister asked me to call you in because he would appreciate your co-operation on one or two small points. (*Pause.*) Regrettably, the Minister himself has just this moment flu —

DANDER. Oh dear. I hope you got him to a doctor.

KLARA. Why should we? He has flu. He is running away.

DANDER. Flown. You mean flown. Flu's 'flu. Influenza. (*Rising.*) What's more I wish to lodge a protest. This goose and its inoffensive owner —

KRK. Sit down McPherson!

DANDER (*sitting*). Dander. (*Plucks at the goose abstractedly.*)

KRK (*snapping his fingers at* KLÁRA). The radio message received by Gustav Turp on the plane, Klára —

She goes through the file and hands over a paper. KRK *studies it a moment, then reads out:*

KRK. 'My author over there McPherson not Dander. Have unfortunately sent Dander to Hollywood in mistake for the twilit Celt. It's an ill wind, Turp. Lucky old you and Klinka have the genius, not the loser. McPherson wrote boffo musical hit on Wop heretic Savonarola and is going for a song, ha-ha, at five thousand dollars a week. Never be shy of pushing your luck with yours truly and as ever — Nathaniel Bunce'.

DANDER. Yes. That sounds authentic.

KRK (*smiling*). In which case Mr McPherson you can hardly be the son of one Heini Dindl! Of course this is no news to you, but the error might have caused you some inconvenience. (*Thwacks the bag.*) The Tokyo despatches require Dander. You are the intrepid Scot. Hájek and others insisted you are Dander. Thus we may demonstrate the great Cambridge mole himself is dangerously incompetent. (*Smugly.*) And we have his arse on a griddle.

DANDER. Er — my passport insists I'm Dander as well. No news to you I'm sure. But the error —

KRK. Please, McPherson! (*Comes round the desk to* DANDER *smiling.*) When I saw how adroitly you coaxed us through the jackal Hájek's web of conspiracy and intrigue — the false passport fell into place at once, you might say. (*Squeezes* DANDER'S *shoulder.*) We know somebody in your London section's been after Hájek for years. How fortunately all our interests coincide! (*He makes a sign to* KLÁRA.) Want to see something?

KLÁRA *presses a switch. The gauze wall is illuminated. On the other side, brilliantly lit, in handcuffs and gagged with elastoplast:* HÁJEK; KLINKA; LUDMILA; TURP; *the* YOUNG MAN; *the* PEASANT WOMAN *and the two* HEAVIES. *All sit in a row bolt upright on wooden chairs facing downstage.*

DANDER. I wonder what Lenin would have made of it all?

KRK. You don't think it began with Stalin, do you? There's a historical line stretching back from this building all the way to the Romanovs. Further, I shouldn't be surprised.

DANDER. Well you can release the old peasant lady and the boy, to start with. And give her back this goose will you?

KRK. See to it at once, Klára.

She gingerly takes the goose from DANDER *and goes off. We shall see her on the other side of the 'wall' with a* GUARD — *who releases the* PEASANT *and the* YOUNG MAN *and leads them away.*

DANDER. Now. I don't know what your Minister had in mind for me before he flew, but Klinka and his wife and Turp —

KRK. Please to hold your horses, my friend. All we ask from your people in London is they get Dander from Los Angeles to Prague.

Pause.

DANDER. Krk. You want to put the lever on Heini Dindl too?

KRK (*acidly*). You object? So forget it. (KLÁRA *enters.*) Klára we interrogate that scum and find the whereabouts of Jaroslav Klumm. We fly Klumm to Japan where he will identify Dindl. We shoot Klumm. We kick the shit out of Dindl till he buys his life with those ill-gotten gains. That's one scenario.

DANDER. I had to dispose of Klumm yesterday. Keep it under your hat. My own masters aren't wild about open government either. You release the three I named — you get Dander. That's another scenario.

KRK slumps into his chair visibly deflated. KLÁRA goes to him and takes his hand.

KRK. How else to get that little farm in West Virginia, Klára?

DANDER. Unless I underestimate Bunce completely, he's sent Dander to Hollywood to write a screenplay for Louis Beaney. Suppose you invite Beaney to Karlovy Vary? Add to that it's supposed to be me that's writing the screenplay anyway. He'll be outraged when he gets Dander.

KRK. Dander can't write?

DANDER. Let me put it this way. He's no McPherson.

KRK. And what about Beaney's self-esteem? To be invited at the last moment? He is old. Famous. Drowning already in prizes and honours.

DANDER (*rising to go*). Suit yourself —

KRK (*shuffling papers*). Klumm was still on the payroll when I took over. (*Shuffling.*) Hájek's payroll needless to say. (*Sits back exhausted.*) You know the defecting Minister's crime, McPherson?

DANDER. What?

KRK. Secretiveness. I'm frightened out of my wits myself. Once upon a time there was a Klumm. Now there isn't. Sudden death. Disappearance. Time was I only jumped when I hear somebody's still around. Our own people. Your people. KGB. CIA. Do we ever know the game they're playing upstairs, McPherson? Pawns like you and me? (*Mops his brow.*) All I want is to die with my scalp on in the good old USA. (*Looks at the prisoners, shudders and switches off the light that makes the 'wall' transparent.*) Klára. Dare we do what he asks?

KLÁRA. Well, Comrade Krk —

KRK. Be bold, my darling. Be bold.

KLÁRA. Filmexport already complain that we hold Turp —

KRK. Fine, fine —

KLÁRA. I should explain to Mr McPherson —

KRK. Spit it out, woman!

KLÁRA. Just as the Americans have token blacks in the system, we have token free people. (*Timidly.*) I think Comrade Krk in his zeal to crush the jackal Hájek forgot Klinka and his wife are technically in this token free category. (*Half-curtsies to* KRK.) Excuse me, Tonda —

KRK. Right. Okay. They're yours, McPherson. On one condition.

DANDER. Yes?

KRK. You all four go to Karlovy Vary and wait. Klára, you get Karlovy Vary to wire Beaney. (*Shouting as she hovers.*) Now! (KLÁRA *goes.*) I just want to make one thing clear, McPherson. (*Come out from behind the desk.*) I don't have Dander, I've nothing to screw Dindl with. For the boy, he might talk. Now two million might be nothing to the idealistic type of agent like yourself. Me, if I don't get it there's going to be a purge in this country it'll make the Kremlin seem like the Friends of the Earth. Get it? And you'll be the first to go. (*Pause.*) You'd better deliver.

DANDER. I think London wants Hájek sacked, by the way. Not cremated.

KRK (*touches the zipper of his flies*). You want my balls? What's the matter with you people?

DANDER. All part of the Grand Design, Krk. Us. Washington. Moscow. Paris. Bonn. East Berlin. You know the kind of thing.

KRK (*shouting*). I don't want to know! I want to be a rich farmer in Virginia — right?

DANDER. What makes you think Heini Dindl's still got the money?

KRK *rolls his eyes upwards and crosses his fingers.* DANDER *starts to leave.*

KRK. What makes you think Beaney'll bring Dander? Why should he?

DANDER *rolls his eyes upwards and crosses his fingers.* KRK *grins.*

KRK. Ciao baby —

DANDER. Ciao —

DANDER *goes.* KRK *crosses to the Lenin pedestal. He kicks it hard and the bust falls off.*

Fade out.

Fade in:

Scene Three

A hotel room in Karlovy Vary. The following evening. Faint music.
Coloured lights play outside.
   LUDMILA *sprawls on a chaise-longue in a smart dress.* KLINKA
and DANDER *are in chairs. All have drinks.*

KLINKA (*raising his glass*). Here is to you, Horatio. We wish also
   to thank you for what you did for us yesterday. Na zdravi!

ALL. Na zdraví!

LUDMILA. I think he makes a charming secret agent.

KLINKA (*crossing to the window*). And how do you like Karlovy
   Vary?

DANDER. It makes me feel like two million dollars.

KLINKA. Forgive me, Horatio. I am not insensitive to your
   predicament.

DANDER (*to* KLINKA). I wonder what you'd have been like in
   the West?

LUDMILA. Greedy.

DANDER. I do wish you'd try not to be so awful to each other.

LUDMILA. The story goes that when Jirka was six years old, a
   school inspector asked him what he wanted to be when he grew
   up. Little Klinka turned his big wide eyes up to the man and said —

DANDER. A film director?

LUDMILA. An egoist.

KLINKA. Ludmila! Please —

DANDER. You both seem very conveniently to have forgotten —

KLINKA. What, my boy?

DANDER. That no way can I get McPherson-alias-Dander here,
   even if Beaney's vain enough to accept their insultingly last-
   minute invitation. (*Drinks.*) And even if I could, what sort of
   bastard would land McPherson in the shit like that? (*Drinks.*)
   And if I did — then I'm no better than the rest of you.

LUDMILA. Voops!

DANDER. Yes? Voops?

KLINKA (*sadly, turns to the window*). She and Beaney were lovers once. For three days at the Venice Film Festival many years ago. (*Pause.*) She telephoned him in Los Angeles before we all left Prague yesterday.

DANDER. He must have been pretty ancient, however long ago it was. I'll bet he's eighty by now if he's a day.

KLINKA (*quietly, to the window*). Seventy-three.

LUDMILA. Ah, Horatio. You can't imagine how beautiful it was. I could not believe this . . . this master . . . could even notice a little girl from Cechoslovakia. (*Touches her cheeks.*) How ugly I become since then! You notice that motherfucker Turp did not recognise me yesterday morning? He was in Venice when Louis Beaney and I —

DANDER. Would you please just give me the gist of the conversation?

LUDMILA *gets up and sways about triumphantly with her drink. She pouts at* DANDER *and tickles his ear.*

LUDMILA. Louis will come to Karlovy Vary. Yesterday. At once. (*Dreamily.*) For me. Only for me. (*Pause.*) I cried a little —

DANDER. I once heard Bunce say Beaney's drunk half the time.

LUDMILA. All the time.

DANDER. Was he drunk on the phone?

LUDMILA. Smashed like crazy.

DANDER. Well that's some bloody use, I must say.

LUDMILA. Yes it is. Louis drinks only to bring out the best in himself. It is when he is drunk his imagination is on fire. His memories live. (*Drinks.*) Also then he keeps his word. Does what he says he will do.

DANDER (*glumly*). Some of us are like that brutally sober.

LUDMILA. He brings the true McPherson with him, my darling. If he has to drug him, he said.

DANDER. McPherson was drugged all the time at Oxford.

LUDMILA. Well so now what do you think of your Ludmila?

DANDER. You've saved my bacon all right. But I'm afraid Comrade Krk'll smoke McPherson's. (*Crossing to* KLINKA.) Jirka. What's a token free person?

KLINKA (*turning mournfully*). It is one for whom compromise has no end, Horatio. No limits. No bottom. (*Pause.*) It is a secret official category, but known by that phrase only in Prague cafés I believe. (*Very quietly, and touching* DANDER'S *arm gently.*) You have joined us — no? (*He puts his arms round* DANDER, *who jumps back.*)

DANDER. No!

KLINKA. Shssh, Horatio. You have been like a son to me.

DANDER. D'you think I lied and made that deal with Krk to save you *personally?* It was a question of —

KLINKA. Yes? Of what?

DANDER. I mean, don't you think the difference between people like you and my alleged father is really just one of *scale?*

Pause.

KLINKA. Perhaps. (*Leaving.*) In which case I think you have made an important discovery, my friend. (*Goes.*)

DANDER *stands transfixed and bewildered.* LUDMILA *stretches out on the chaise-longue.*

LUDMILA. Are you going to make love to me Horatio?

DANDER. In the circumstances I think that's a disgusting proposal!

He stalks to the door and flings it open. HÁJEK *breezes in pushing a trolley: champagne, flowers, a dish of hors d'oeuvres.*

HÁJEK. Compliments of the mangement, Horrors. (*He swoops on* LUDMILA *and kisses her hand.*) Klinková, I am your slave —

DANDER. What are you doing here?

HÁJEK. After your brilliant coup in getting us off the hook I volunteered — so to say — for humble menial work. (*Uncorks the champagne.*) Don't you think I displayed remarkable presence of mind? Otherwise I might have been digging uranium next week. Oh what a tick is Comrade Krk! An absolute nobody till yesterday. Counter-espionagewise, the owl of the remove. (*Pouring.*) So it goes Dander. Snakes and ladders. Up with one Minister and down with the next. Horrors you can't imagine how relieved I was on your behalf to hear Beaney and McPherson are on their way.

DANDER. Oh yes? How did you hear?

HÁJEK *switches on an overhead light. As they look up, the lightfitting slides up and down several inches.*

HÁJEK. Yes, dear heart. It's my boys up there. Krk sent them
into social exile with me. By gum you've unnerved them in
Prague old son, Shaken them till their iron maidens rattle. The
faction now beavering to depose Krk refers to you as the
monster of Karlovy Vary. (*Feels in his pocket.*) However, I like
to keep my hand in while the wheel turns. And whilst Comrade
Krk scampers on the treadmill — your man in the department
has not come away empty-handed. (*Waves two passports.*)
Voilà! American passports for the Klinkas. Dated. Valid.
Photos. The lot. It's a sort of understanding we have with the
CIA. Originally these belonged to a couple of their spooks we
knocked off for Washington. The routine under my previous
minister was to have Western passports stashed away for emer-
gencies. (*At* LUDMILA.) Token free persons a special category.
(*Drinks.*) And there they were snug in his safe when I borrowed
them as I quit the ship of state. (*Grins.*) Severance pay, if you like.
(*To* DANDER.) Fifteen thousand dollars a piece, chico.

DANDER. I don't get it.

HÁJEK. You want the Klinkas out, don't you?

LUDMILA. He'd better.

DANDER. Now just a minute —

HÁJEK. Oh, Horrors! When McPherson arrives, Krk will grab him
under the impression he's Dander. Yes? And by the time he's
established McPherson's bona fides Krk's going to be after you
with murder on his heart — no?

DANDER. The thought had crossed my mind.

HÁJEK. You're coming on, Dander! So. In the little meantime we
have, you could be on your way to twist your daddy's arm up
there on his crag in Japan. Don't you think it's awe-inspiringly
neat? (*Pulls out an Australian passport.*) Mine's Australian and
I'm off to Sydney. When I get my thirty thousand dollars there
from you, Horatio — the passports will be delivered to the
Klinkas here. (*Drinks.*) They'll be out home and dry before you
can say negation of the negation.

DANDER. Given up your own ambitions for Dindl's gold, have you?

HÁJEK. A political security officer who loses out in Prague,
Horrors, loses his all. If you hadn't kindly put in a word for me
with Krk, I'd be a concrete stanchion in the new Metro by now.

DANDER (*firmly*). I won't do it.

HÁJEK (*At* LUDMILA). You're screwing her aren't you? Besides,

I thought you'd come here touring your conscience? I thought you were a sort freedom fighter in your own Peter Pannish little way. (*Flouncing off.*) I don't care —

DANDER. I was going to tell you a thing or two about yourself in the park, Hájek. I think I'd better get it over with now —

The light comes down over DANDER'S head as if listening. Infuriated, he grabs it with both hands by the flex and jerks. Lamp and flex come down in his hands. Chunks and clouds of plaster shower over him. There is a loud cracking noise and HÁJEK'S HEAVIES — in dirty boiler suits — crash to the floor at DANDER'S feet. He helps them up, brushing at the plaster. They stand bashfully, heads down, to receive HÁJEK'S wrath.

HÁJEK (*icily*). Tweedledumnik and Tweedledeenik! Clean it up! (*Roaring it in Czech.*) Clean it up! (*They scurry out.*) Moscow-trained, it goes without saying. (*Reaching for his glass, he drinks.*) Give them a fresh start and they fall arse over tit in it. Do tell Horrors how much you want him, Ludmila.

The HEAVIES re-enter with brushes, dustpans, buckets. They creep about cleaning up the mess. LUDMILA stares at DANDER disdainfully.

LUDMILA. I can't wait to have you by my side for ever, Horatio. Humming 'Guantanamera' in bed. Whispering sweet dialectics. Telling me what went wrong after nineteen seventeen. Where and when and how. (*Drily to HÁJEK.*) No, Hájek darling. I think we shall have to try Louis Beaney. He's loaded. He's sentimental. And he's had it in for communism ever since McCarthy threw him out of the States.

HÁJEK (*snaps his fingers*). Bingo! (*Goes off jauntily.*)

One of the HEAVIES timidly approaches LUDMILA and whispers in her ear. She bursts out laughing.

DANDER. Now what?

LUDMILA. They have a message for you from Comrade Krk. (*Pause: laughing.*) Watch it, McPherson!

DANDER (*As JANA enters*). They've deserted Hájek?

LUDMILA. Mentally.

DANDER. They've changed sides?

JANA. That's what seems to keep everybody happy, Misha.

Blackout.

Fade in:

Scene Four

A hotel terrace in Karlovy Vary. The next morning. TURP — *in open-necked shirt, cravat, slacks, yellow casuals* — *is being served coffee by* KLUMM *in his waiter's gear. Other* WAITERS *are moving about lazily doing various jobs and setting up tables for the opening of the festival* — *each one with a small foreign flag.*

TURP *takes a ten dollar bill and a sheaf of postcard-sized photos from his jacket, which hangs on the chair.*

TURP (*thrusting the bill into* KLUMM'S *pocket*). Name?

KLUMM. Klumm, Sir.

TURP (*passing the photos*). That's a ten dollar bill. Grab these. Now every one of them's a famous person in the film business. You savvy?

KLUMM. So?

TURP. So when the film festival opens tonight, you see one of these schnorrers in the bar, the foyer — you have me paged. Turp. Gustav Turp. All righty?

KLUMM (*examines the photos*). You seen what's with the dollar lately?

TURP. You are a sample of communism?

KLUMM. Straight down the line.

TURP. Where were you born sonny?

KLUMM. Here and there.

TURP. You look Turkish to me. I didn't know there was any Turks in Poland.

KLUMM. I have cousins in Moravska-Ostrava.

TURP. You gastarbeiter, Klumm? They fly you in from Instanbul? My folks came from Smyrna. Back in Smyrna we used to chew Turks like pretzels. (*Leans back shading his eyes.*) What a hole for a film festival! You see those people down there in the street? Walking up and down sucking things like mini-pisspots? What is it — the local fetish?

KLUMM. They take the waters, Herr Turp. Karlovy Vary is also famous for its healing waters.

TURP. You give me any more of that 'herr' shit and I'll take
you apart. Small and fat as I am. I'll ramm you back in your
goddamn fez and kick you all the way to Mecca. You fancy
a pilgrimage?

KLUMM (*puts the photos away*). I'll take twenty dollars.

TURP (*slaps down another bill*). Done.

> KLUMM *takes the money and goes.* TURP *sips his coffee,
> grimacing. Takes a copy of 'Variety' from his pocket and starts
> reading. Distant loudspeakers hiccup music from time to time.*
> KLINKA *enters and ostentatiously takes another table. Orders
> coffee.*

TURP. You got to get out of this low mood Jeery. People screw
my wife all the time. I send them scorpions.

KLINKA. You do — what?

TURP. Mail them to the offending cuckoos in little boxes. Have
you any idea what those goddamn insects cost? But the way I
look at it, money's no object when there's an alien tool in my
Laura.

KLINKA. Nobody's screwing my wife.

TURP. No more films behind the iron curtain for Old Gus. He's up
to here. (*Shakes the paper.*) So who comes to Varlovy Kary?
Reds? Weirdos? Nobodies? You tell me. But first let me tell
you: my family had all the shit it could take back in Odessa.

KLINKA. I thought it was Kiev.

TURP. One of those places. Where's McPherson if he's not with
Madame? I thought we had a script conference?

KLINKA. You still wish to go ahead? After yesterday's
humiliations?

TURP. So they made me sign a paper I was in the zoo all day.
Okay. I was in the zoo. (*Pause.*) Humiliation? Jeery you don't
know what it is. You been spoon-fed with all this socialism,
right? You don't know capitalism. The cheating, the treachery.
The heartbreaks. Old Gus sucked humiliation at the tit. I eat it.
I breathe it all my life. I get ahead on humiliation. Without it
what am I? I'll tell you a secret, friend. Humiliation builds
character. Look at Bunce. He moves heaven and earth to get
McPherson into my stable. And it's not just the ten per cent,
Jeery. It's the prestige. (*Reading.*) What's this? You read
Variety? Listen: In Hollywood this week. Braw Scottish

playwright Rory McPherson to script his smash-hit musical *A Ring of Fire* for maverick Louis Beaney. Asked about the new wave of gutsy young playwrights currently snapping at the heels of the British establishment, McPherson said: The only new writer with talent on the London scene is my old friend and contemporary at Oxford, Horatio Dander.' (*Pause.*) He said that about McPherson? I mean Dander? Jesus what a tribute to the old Turp flair. Makes a man feel you know? Trandenscental. Go find him Jeery will you? Ask him what I'm paying him two hundred a week for. To poke your wife?

KLINKA. Gottes Willen I just had breakfast with him and Ludmila! In separate rooms, you filth.

TURP. I have to lay it on the line, Jeery. Who dragged that dumb freak out of the gutter? Right. Old Gus. (*Lowering the paper.*) Still and all. McPherson would have had the edge in the international market.

KLINKA. Then you may be consoled to know that Beaney is coming to Czechoslovakia and bringing McPherson with him.

TURP (*studies his fingernails*). You must have been a nice kid once, Jeery. It's not your fault you shrink when I'm in frame. They screw all night and you snatch the tab for two breakfasts? You're a broken man. You could never direct this film in a million years. Come to that. You seen Beaney's *Never In a Million Years*? What a movie! (*Dreamily.*) Now, Beaney and McPherson. That's a package.

KLINKA. I thought you just wished me to re-hire Horatio?

TURP. He has the chutzpah to let me think he's McPherson? He can't get away with it. Re-fire the little bastard.

KLINKA. I must inform you. You cannot fire me.

TURP. Inside my head Jeery, I just did.

KLINKA. This is a people's democracy. About the only thing you can fire somebody here for is telling the truth. (*Pause.*) I had meant to say —

TURP. That's right cookie. You just qualified. So now get your Jewish ass out of town, will you?

KLINKA. And who is a Jew also?

TURP. There's yids and yids.

KLINKA (*shouting*). I'll have you extradited!

TURP. I was born extradited. You think I can't square these
amateurs? Blindfold I can do it, with hard currency. The
commy jail doesn't exist that can hold Gustav Amadeus Turp.
I got more well-greased fingers than your government's got
arseholes. I really mean that. If you'd made *Never in a Million
Years* now. That was a movie.

KLINKA. It was a satire on socialism in the Soviet Union, you
idiot.

TURP. Made *Gone With the Wind* look like a mousefart, anyhow.

KLINKA. Meshugge!

TURP. Shmockeroony!

KLINKA. Back to the shtetl, scheisse!

TURP. And where did your mother crawl from? A pig's belly in
the Ukraine?

Furiously, KLINKA *starts throwing everything in sight at*
TURP: *cups, saucers, coffee pot, milk jug, salt and pepper.*
TURP *retreats shielding his face with his arms.*

Fade out

Fade in:

Scene Five

Hotel terrace. Dusk.
    HÁJEK, *in his waiter's jacket and black trousers, is directing
unseen technicians. He stands with his hands on his hips looking
upwards while unintelligible Czech voices crackle through the
loudspeaker system. He points to a table.*

HÁJEK. Tady?

LOUDSPEAKERS. Ano.

    HÁJEK *sits. He is flooded by a spotlight. A few bars of the*
Marseillaise. *When the music stops,* HÁJEK *gets up and goes to
another table.*

HÁJEK. Tady?

LOUDSPEAKERS. Ano.

HÁJEK *sits. A few bars of* Old Glory. *A babble of electronic voices. Fragments of other national anthems. Silence.* DANDER *enters.*

DANDER. What's going on?

HÁJEK. Rehearsals, dear boy. Their idea of a festival reception. Every distinguished foreigner gets a spotlight and the appropriate national anthem. (*Pause.*) We've a lot to learn, Horrors. We've only been a backward country since nineteen forty-eight. (*He fusses about at the tables.*) Tonight'll be a disaster, of course. This hotel's staffed entirely with superannuated spies and disgraced intellectuals. (KRK *enters with* JANA — HÁJEK *makes a camply haughty exit.*) Excuse me! His grace the duke of Prague, and companion —

KRK *and* JANA *go straight to* DANDER, *who has reeled in shock and fear to a chair and sits trembling.*

KRK (*beaming*). Rory my dear boy — you are a miracle worker! (*Sits, patting* DANDER'S *sleeve and chuckling.*) Beaney arrives to Prague this afternoon with Dander. We arrest the impostor. Beaney storms and makes the fuss. Dander hysterical — we drug him. Jana drives the now drunken Beaney to Karlovy Vary this afternoon (*To* JANA.) — but you have told Rory already, no?

DANDER. She tried. I'm afraid my ceiling had just fallen in on me.

KRK. How did you do it?

DANDER. I just happened to be swinging on this lamp, and —

KRK. No no no. How did you pull it off, to give me Dander on a plate? You have impressed me McPherson, you really have. This afternoon I take the decision of my life. Klára waits with two of my best men and Dander at a military airport not so far away. She keeps him under the drug. (*Smiling happily.*) When he wakes we are all in Japan, sniffing the almond blossom ! From there we shall play it by ear.

DANDER. How do you mean?

KRK. I mean we shall find where Dindl hides and post him one of Dander's ears. He is a dangerous man. He half killed two of that swine Hájek's agents (*Pause.*) Jana, he is crying! Why do you weep, McPherson? You have a squeasy stomach for the son of a war criminal?

DANDER. As a matter of fact — yes. I mean, young Dander's everybody's mug in this scenario isn't he? Don't you dare cut his ears off!

KRK (*rising*). You know? We always found your London section quite incomprehensible. When I left Prague they were affecting to know nothing about this whole operation. And such a subtle one, too. (*He chucks* DANDER'S *cheek smiling.*) Ah what a nation of hypocrites! But it leads to brilliance in our profession. (*Puts his hands on* DANDER'S *shoulders, raising him up.*) Sorry to say, I must go at once Rory. (*Kisses* DANDER'S *cheeks.*) Goodbye — and thank you.

As he goes he is caught in a spot and there are a few stuttering bars of some national anthem. Music and light are killed when KRK *shakes his fist.*
DANDER *eyes* JANA *numbly.*

DANDER. Off with the old and on with the new so quickly?

JANA. Well, Misha. That's —

TOGETHER. What seems to keep everybody happy.

Pause

JANA. Who knows? When Krk is replaced, perhaps I shall be the next Klára.

DANDER. Who'll be the next Krk? Any idea?

JANA. I just wished to say I am very attached to you Misha. Perhaps it is I still have a weakness in me for the human anachronism. If I were not a career girl, I'd gladly run to England with you —

DANDER. I said: Who'll be the next Krk?

Pause

JANA. Jaroslav Klumm.

Pause

DANDER. I see. (*Pause.*) There's something wonderfully inevitable about it all, isn't there.

JANA. The Grand Design, Misha.

DANDER. My very words to Krk.

JANA. Klumm has had Krk's office bugged ever since Hájek was arrested. (*Coughs apologetically.*) His men are waiting for Krk at the military airport. They will arrest him and Klára, and take over Operation Codename Dindl Swindle for Klumm. (*Pause.*) If I were you Misha, I'd get out of Karlovy Vary tonight. (*Pause.*) Will you kiss me? I have to go —

DANDER. I'd rather kiss a warthog's arse.

JANA (*shouting*). You can talk! Who got the innocent McPherson into this mess?

DANDER (*blandly*). He always did have unsightly ears.

JANA *stalks off, chased by a spot and a few ragged bars of a national anthem.*

DANDER. Slivovici prosím!

He sits hunched and wretched. A WAITER *brings the drink.* KLINKA *enters. He has a dramatic black eye, and carries a bottle of Slivovice.*

KLINKA. Horatio. Where have you been all day?

DANDER. Looking into your beautiful black eye — hiding.

KLINKA (*sits, pours a drink*). You should see what I did to Old Gus. I bent his hooter and no mistaking. (*Drinks.*) He has the mouth of a Tel Aviv taxi-driver. What's more he is trying to get us both off the picture. The studio tells me yes, I cannot be sacked — but it happens they have found for me a wonderful documentary. Forty minutes on the life of some damned ornithologist in the Tatras. (*Drinks.*) We get the message. (*Expansively.*) Danderle! How good to sit and drink with you before the crowds arrive. My own son is fat, mean, humourless and safely studies microbiology. (*Thumps* DANDER'S *back.*) You! Your tender heart and bewildering political delusions — they charm the arse off me.

DANDER. Jirka —

KLINKA. For you, anything mein Lieber —

DANDER. Has your brain got an instant wiping mechanism? Like a tape recorder?

KLINKA. We all acquire one sooner or later Horatio. How's yours coming along?

DANDER. Are there any decently high bridges in Karlovy Vary?

KLINKA (*hasn't heard*). Ah, the sun sinks low. And I, Jiří Klinka — veteran of so many regimes — I fear I go down with the sun, Horatio. (*Pause.*) Think of it. When my plane touched down in forty-five I was a hero. Strutting about in a nice blue RAF uniform. Kissing Russians. (*Pause.*) Everything was so clear in the war. We knew the enemy, then. (*Hums the opening of Beethoven's Fifth.*) Di di di dee. Da da da daa. (*Pause.*)

That great music. The call-sign of liberty for the partisans, for the resistance everywhere. (*Pulls himself together and thumps DANDER'S back, grinning.*) And then there I was. Just one more foolish monomaniac with his head full of celluloid plans —

DANDER. Jirka —

KLINKA. Shsssh —

He puts his finger to his lips and his eyes follow TURP — *who enters pursued by a spot and a bar or two of* Greensleeves. *He has a plaster across his nose. He ignores* DANDER *and* KLINKA, *to sit at another table.*

KLINKA (*crooning softly*). Ach, mein liebe turpen-tine, tur-pentine tur-pentine —

TURP (*stomps over to* KLINKA). Did you get a spot? Did you get music?

KLINKA (*standing*). Světla! Hudba!

KLINKA is instantly awash in a spotlight. The speakers boom out the first line of Speed bonny boat/Like a bird on the wing/ Over the sea to Skye.

TURP. Somebody up there still thinks you're McPherson, Dander —

He goes back to his table chuckling, as DANDER *grabs* KLINKA *by the lapels shouting.*

DANDER. Klumm's still alive and he *knows* I'm Dander!

The speakers blare out the Internationale. LOUIS BEANEY *enters with* LUDMILA. *He is a tall, heavy, grand sort of person in an olive-green safari suit. They are caught startled and blinking as the* Internationale *switches to* Old Glory. *As the music falters and fades,* BEANEY *strides over to* DANDER, *who is still clutching at* KLINKA.

BEANEY. You Dander?

KLINKA (*standing, shaking* DANDER *off*). Maître! Looking into your beautiful blue eyes, he is already working on a script of my own.

BEANEY. Shut up, Fiasco. Cool it. (*Booming at* DANDER.) Loodie there tells me you're a useless prick if ever there was one Dander.

DANDER. I don't think my ineptitude's quite up to that of certain shots in *Never in a Million Years*. Nevertheless, I —

BEANEY. Never say 'I' to me boy. I'll tell you what you are.
You're one of those frigging whore's chancres the womb of the
west seems to be coughing out by the thousand these days.
Baader-Meinhof. Red faction, fraction, God knows what.
Can't you keep your ugly mits off a genuinely degraded
workers' state?

TURP (*rising, waves diffidently*). Hi there, Louis —

BEANEY'S *eyes swivel till they find* TURP. *They fix him with
leonine contempt.*

BEANEY (*grimly*). Remember that time you got into an elevator
in Venice with me and Fellini, Turp?

TURP. Why sure I do, Louis. I was just (saying the other day) —

BEANEY. And you — you dared to greet me? (*As* TURP *nods,
petrified.*) What did I say?

TURP (*croaking*). Never in private, Gus. Never in private —

BEANEY. So frig off then, will you? Your goddamn nose is using
my air. (*Rounds on* DANDER *as* TURP *creeps away.*) Christ
knows, Dander. We had a few mothers like you in the Thirties
but they were genuine idealists. (*Roaring.*) Where *is* my frigging
screenwriter? Has your spineless generation not got one
goddamn thing going for it?

Pause

DANDER (*firm and clear*). Resistance —

KLUMM *and* HAJEK *have entered unobtrusively to stand
motionless at the opposite side of the stage. The speakers blare
out the Japanese national anthem.
A tall, shaven-headed monk* (DINDL) *enters dressed in a saffron
robe. For a long moment he is caught in the full brilliance of
the spot. The music ends abruptly.* DINDL *comes slowly
downstage towards* DANDER *and stops a few paces away from
him.*

DINDL (*gently*). Horacio?

The two look at each other a moment. Slowly, DANDER
turns his back on DINDL. DINDL *looks towards* KLUMM,
who has a gun trained on him.

DINDL. What can I say, Horacio? What you must have heard of me
is true. (*Pause.*) I can only say I met your mother when I was
at the heart of my consuming shame. (*Pause.*) When you were
born, I loved you from the first moment. I have since come to

believe my own soul was born then too. (*To* ALL:) Whoever and whatever you all may be — and I have neither the interest nor means to judge — this man (*Points at* KLUMM.) belongs only to himself. To me the idea of self is now ludicrous. But that is another matter. (*Pause.*) Have you learned anything, Horacio?

DINDL sees KLUMM raise his gun. DANDER leaps forward, bringing his hand down on KLUMM'S wrist.
There are bursts of machine-pistol fire from all sides, and pandemonium breaks out. Spotlights flash on and off, there are wild bursts of music from the speakers. KLUMM, DINDL and DANDER are left dying. Only KLINKA remains with them on the stage.
KLINKA goes to DANDER'S body and raises it a little in his arms, hugging it. He is weeping.

KLINKA. Horatio? (*Pause.*) Horatio?

Fade out.

Fade in:

Scene Six

A café in Prague. Some months later.
  The setting is a replica of Scene Two.
  KLINKA, with a SOUND MAN and a CAMERAMAN with a hand-held camera, has been directing.
  KLINKA now takes a hand-mike. The CAMERAMAN films him speaking.

KLINKA. From this cellar in a suburb of Prague, you have seen some of our comrades and heard their statements. (*Pause.*) We hope this will be only the first of many underground films we shall try to bring to people in all countries. (*Pause.*) The young man whose tragic death was so cynically presented to the world media some weeks ago, died in my arms not far from this place. (*Pause.*) I found in his coat a fragment of prose and a choreographic sketch. (*Pause.*) It was signed: The monster of Karlovy Vary. (*Pause.*) I wish to read out this fragment, then to end this film with Horatio Dander's one and only contribution to the cinema. (*Takes out a piece of paper and reads*) 'Not only have our words but even our colours become your lies. You have torn the red flag from our hearts and unfurled it over imprisoned nations. (*Pause.*) You have stolen the gentle black of peaceful anarchy and out it into uniforms. (*Pause.*) You have locked our human poetry in steel.'

The light fades on KLINKA. *Another fades up on a* YOUNG MAN *and a* YOUNG WOMAN — *both crouching naked, their wrists and ankles fettered in bright steel chains, their eyes and mouths in silver cloth.*

A loudspeaker begins to play edited sections of Beethoven's Fifth Symphony.

The young people mime agonised bondage, anger, struggle. Finally they break the fetters and free their eyes and mouths. At this point they arrive naked, humble, heads bowed, arms spread wide, downstage.

As the light fades on them, we hear the loud blare of rising and falling police-car sirens.

Blackout.

End.

THEN AND NOW

List of Characters

JOHN BAILDON

MRS BAILDON (His mother)

JAMES FENWICK

ISABEL FENWICK (His daughter)

EMMA BAILDON

ROBERT (Emma's brother)

Act One

Scene One

The kitchen/living-room of a miner's terrace house in Yorkshire. Early 1945. The wireless is turned on to a war news bulletin.

JOHN BAILDON, a young Green Howards captain, stands by the range listening. He has a silver whiskey flask in one hand. One arm in a black silk sling.

MRS BAILDON, his mother, sits at the table pouring tea. JOHN turns off the wireless. He goes to pour whiskey into her tea. She pushes his arm away.

MRS BAILDON. Nay.

There is a silence. He pours whiskey into his own tea.

MRS BAILDON. I'd have thought your mother deserved better.

JOHN. Than what?

MRS BAILDON. Than coming like this in a rush between one train and the next.

Pause.

JOHN. You look well in black.

MRS BAILDON. That's some consolation then.

Pause.

JOHN. I wish I could have been here, mother.

MRS BAILDON. It were my first new frock in two years.

Pause.

JOHN. What happened exactly? Down the pit.

MRS BAILDON. There were an explosion. Then it flooded. (*Pause.*) They sealed it off, in the end.

JOHN. It makes you shiver. It must have happened the same day I got wounded.

MRS BAILDON. The Lord giveth, and the Lord taketh away.

JOHN. You don't believe that bloody rubbish.

Pause.

MRS BAILDON. No. I don't.

JOHN. It's time you got out of black, if you ask me.

There is a colander of runner beans on the table. She begins to top and tail them.

MRS BAILDON. I wear black because I'm bitter, young man. (*Pause.*) Let the neighbours think it's for mourning. (*Pause.*) I'm glad you weren't here. A funeral service for six men lying down there in a flooded seam. It were right strange. (*Pause.*) No coffins. (*Pause.*) Flowers though, aye. A lot of flowers.

Pause.

JOHN. I wish I'd been here, though.

Pause.

MRS BAILDON. What do you know? Between yon pit, his union and the Communist Party your dad were no' but a lodger in this house.

Pause.

JOHN. You loved each other.

MRS BAILDON. I don't know as I believe in that bloody rubbish either.

JOHN. Nay. Come on.

MRS BAILDON. I don't know what I'm doing these for. Who's going to eat them? Our Brian can't bide runner beans. (*Pause.*) You could have stayed on to see him. (*Pause.*) If Brian hadn't gone down t'pit as well, you'd never have seen the inside of yon grammar school.

JOHN. That's right.

MRS BAILDON. It's a miracle he weren't on the same shift as your dad.

JOHN. Where is he this evening, anyway?

MRS BAILDON. Drinking his damned head off in Pontefract if I know him. With some land-girl he's courting. (*Pause.*) Between the pair of you I sometimes wonder what I've gotten.

JOHN. Mam. I was nearly killed in France, you know.

MRS BAILDON. I know.

JOHN. Well thanks!

Pause.

MRS BAILDON. How old is this lass you're off up to see in Northumberland?

JOHN. Seventeen.

MRS BAILDON. I thought most on them big houses had been taken over for t'duration.

JOHN. That's right. They've got the RAF.

MRS BAILDON. What sort on a place is it, then?

Pause.

JOHN. A castle. As a matter of fact.

MRS BAILDON. Oh aye? And I suppose she's t'sleeping beauty?

JOHN. That's right.

Pause.

MRS BAILDON. You want your head examining.

JOHN. I've had it examined. A piece of shrapnel went right through it. (*Pause.*) Are you totally inhuman?

MRS BAILDON. A castle. (*Pause.*) It would've right amused your father.

JOHN. Choked him, wouldn't it?

Pause.

MRS BAILDON. She'll be a lady, then.

JOHN. She's a young woman, at any rate.

MRS BAILDON. With a title.

JOHN. Miss.

MRS BAILDON. You want your brains washing.

JOHN. I very nearly had them blown out.

MRS BAILDON. That did happen to one of your father's officers in nineteen seventeen. (*Pause.*) He said the young man's condition afterwards were much the same as it were afore.

Pause.

JOHN. I think I'd better be off.

Pause.

MRS BAILDON. All the same. He were proud on you being an officer.

JOHN. I know.

MRS BAILDON. Aye. (*Pause.*) If you'd gone in the army before Hitler invaded Russia, he'd have said you were fighting for imperialism.

JOHN. Objectively.

MRS BAILDON. I never could grasp the meaning of that word.

He comes close to her.

JOHN. Are you all right, mam?

Pause.

MRS BAILDON (*fingering the sling*). That's a lovely bit of silk. (*Pause.*) Bombazine. (*Pause.*) When I were a lady's maid, we wore bombazine of a Sunday.

Pause.

JOHN. Isabel sent it.

He sits opposite her at the table. A silence.

MRS BAILDON. Forty-eight years old, your dad was. (*Pause.*) Forty-eight.

Pause.

JOHN. It'll all be over in a month or two. (*Pause.*) There'll be elections you know mam. (*Pause.*) There's a lot going to have to change in this country.

MRS BAILDON. Oh aye? An' will socialism invent a pit that doesn't kill miners?

Pause.

JOHN. There's a lot can be done. (*Pause.*) It will be.

MRS BAILDON. Well I'm sure you'll have the chance to say so this weekend. Up at yon castle. (*Pause.*) I expect they own a few pits.

Pause.

JOHN. I'm not a communist, you know.

MRS BAILDON. You'd best not be. (*Pause.*) Even your dad said the best use for the party line'd be to hang them buggers in

King Street. (*Smiles.*) Well at least he never tried to din it into you and your brother.

JOHN. Catch Brian!

MRS BAILDON. Catch you an' all, I should hope. (*Pause.*) Our Brian were born thick and stayed thick. He's nowt but a pit pony wi' a thirst for beer and lasses. (*Pause.*) But he's good to me. He works yon allotment. Something else your dad had no time for.

JOHN. I'd have had time. If it hadn't been for my schoolwork. (*Pause.*) You made a right little prisoner on me, mother.

MRS BAILDON. You got your scholarship. You can take it up when you're demobbed. (*Pause.*) Thank God you've come through this lot.

Pause.

JOHN. There's still the Japanese, you know.

MRS BAILDON. Nay. Not after what you've been through.

JOHN. I've been very lucky.

Pause.

MRS BAILDON. If I'd lost two on my men —

He gets up abruptly and goes to the fire.

JOHN. They'll not send me to the Far East. (*Pause.*) I mean it's not likely, anyway.

MRS BAILDON. They do as they like with us.

Pause.

JOHN. He wore this chair out.

MRS BAILDON. I'm putting by for a new one.

Pause.

JOHN. Not much sentimental about you. Is there?

MRS BAILDON. Women that's frightened o' being widows shouldn't marry colliers.

Pause.

JOHN. You thought you were a cut above him, though.

MRS BAILDON. Let's hope you'll be a cut above all on us.

JOHN. I'm not doing medicine for that, mother.

Pause.

MRS BAILDON. You don't have to go tonight.

JOHN Isabel's meeting me off the train in Newcastle.

Pause.

MRS BAILDON. Well. I suppose them pips on your shoulder's opened a few doors.

JOHN. She's not a snob.

MRS BAILDON. She doesn't have to be.

Pause.

JOHN. Maybe you are.

MRS BAILDON. Oh aye. (*Gestures at the room.*) Look at what I've got to be snotty-nosed on.

He crosses to her and rests his hand lightly on her shoulder.

JOHN. You'll be all right, though?

She shakes his hand off and goes to rake the fire. He sits in her chair, fiddling with a knife. She stands by the fire with folded arms.

MRS BAILDON. Take yoursen off to t'station, John. Get out on my sight. (*Pause.*) If our Brian comes in wi' a bellyful of ale and hears you not stopping, he'll go mad.

Pause.

JOHN. When I were a kid and I'd done something wrong, you used to tell me you'd send me to the bad boys' school. (*Pause.*) Do you remember? (*Pause.*) I used to lie awake half the night crying. (*Pause.*) Then in the morning you'd scrub me with a flannel till my cheeks were stinging. You put me in my suit, and set me down at this table with a slice of bread and a mug of tea.

MRS BAILDON. Not to my recollection I didn't.

Pause.

JOHN. When yon clock comes up to half past eight you used to say, I'm putting you on t'bus for the bad boys' school.

MRS BAILDON. I never did, John.

Pause.

JOHN. Unless, you said — unless you get down on your knees and tell your mam you're sorry.

Pause.

MRS BAILDON. What you raking all this up for?

JOHN. Well. When it came to half past eight. That's what I used to do, didn't I? Get down there and beg you to let me stay.

MRS BAILDON. Nay lad. You're making it up as you go along.

Pause.

JOHN. You've forgotten, then?

MRS BAILDON. I don't know as I can forget what I'm sure I never did.

Pause.

JOHN. When I mentioned Isabel just now, that's what I remembered. (*Pause.*) The bread sticking in my throat. Lifting the mug with both hands, trying to gulp down some tea. (*Pause.*) Watching the hands of that clock ticking round. (*He gets up and scrapes the fireside rug with his shoe.*) I can still remember the feel of this rug on my knees when I went down. (*Pause.*) These clippings. And the smell of it. (*Pause.*) It reeked of pit dust and Sunday dinners. (*Pause.*) I suppose you got some brass off his union? Why don't you buy some clippings and make a new rug?

MRS BAILDON. Don't you dare speak to me like that.

JOHN. It's a relief to be a man at last.

MRS BAILDON. Is that what you are, then? Since you've gotten a tailored uniform and a Sam Brown? And been to war and gotten blown up?

Pause.

JOHN. Yes. That's what I think I am.

MRS BAILDON. Men like your father goes to war every day on their lives. (*Shouting.*) Wi' coal!

Pause.

JOHN. You wanted me out of it. (*Pause.*) I got out.

MRS BAILDON. Does she think it's glamorous, then?

Pause.

JOHN. What?

MRS BAILDON. That fancy lass not out o' school. Does she think it's summat romantic, a miner's son?

JOHN. Don't be daft, mother.

*He finds his cap, his respirator, his greatcoat and a small
valise. Dumps them on a chair.*

MRS BAILDON. You'll find out you've overreached yoursen.

JOHN. Will I?

MRS BAILDON. Does her parents know what you are?

Pause.

JOHN. Her mother's dead.

MRS BAILDON. Her father, then. What's he anyway? A lord?

Pause.

JOHN. Her uncle is.

MRS BAILDON. I wish you could see your face.

JOHN. What?

MRS BAILDON. You look that pleased with yoursen.

Pause.

JOHN. No. (*Pause.*) It's just I'm laughing at you.

*She slaps him hard across the face. He freezes. Then clumsily
begins to sling his respirator and put his cap on. He fumbles
the greatcoat over his good arm and picks up his valise.*

JOHN. This is really why I didn't plan to stop over a day or two.
(*Pause.*) It's you and me. (*Pause.*) Pleased with myself? Mam,
that's been one experience among many that's never been
permitted in this house. It's a wonder Brian and me haven't
turned out two right miserable buggers.

MRS BAILDON. Watch your tongue!

JOHN. I'll wash my mouth out on the train.

*He goes to the door and fumbles it open, then turns to look
at her. A long silence.*

MRS BAILDON. What does that girl think you are, I'd like to
know?

Pause.

JOHN. An officer and a gentleman.

*He goes out. After a moment, she closes the door. She sits
at the table. Suddenly she knocks the colander flying across
the room.*

Scene Two

A comfortable library with a log fire.
     JAMES FENWICK — *a man in his early fifties* — *is pouring sherry for himself and his young daughter* ISABEL. *He is wearing a shabby sweater and slacks.* ISABEL *is in a smart dress of the period.*
     A Mozart horn concerto is playing softly.

FENWICK. Have I see you wearing make-up before, Isabel?

ISABEL. Have you looked before?

     Pause.

FENWICK. Touché.

     Pause.

ISABEL. How do I look?

FENWICK. Fast and furious.

ISABEL. Seriously.

     Pause.

FENWICK. Vaguely — Etruscan.

ISABEL. Bang on!

     Pause.

FENWICK. That expression would be RAF demotic, would it? (*Sips.*) How ugly!

ISABEL. All's fair in a war of nerves.

FENWICK. Is that what we're embarked on?

     Pause.

ISABEL. How was Yugoslavia?

FENWICK. Bad for the rheumatism.

ISABEL. Oh come on, Daddy.

FENWICK. You're quite right. I hate the English deprecating manner myself. (*Pause.*) Have you been swotting up on Yugoslavia?

ISABEL. Did you meet Tito?

FENWICK. I did.

ISABEL. What's he like?

FENWICK. Tough, intelligent, and none too happy about Stalin. (*Raising a finger.*) But you don't know where I've been, remember.

Pause.

ISABEL. John's father was a communist.

FENWICK. Where is the young man? He couldn't possibly drown in five inches of bathwater.

ISABEL. His arm, Daddy.

He crosses to a window and looks out.

FENWICK. It seems quite ludicrous, living in a tower.

ISABEL. Uncle Percy says the RAF'll be moving out before long.

Pause.

FENWICK. Everything back to normal?

ISABEL. Why the sour tone? (*Pause.*) The Japanese?

FENWICK. No. (*Pause.*) I'm always uneasy up here. It's lovely country and all that. But. (*Pause.*) I can't wait to get back to Oxford. (*Sips.*) If the RAF hasn't ruined Oxford as well. (*Pause.*) You can't imagine, Isabel, how absurd I look on the end of a parachute. Not to mention hiking about in those bloody awful mountains.

ISABEL. Haven't a clue what you're talking about, of course.

Pause.

FENWICK. Isabel. What are you going to do?

ISABEL. Do you mean John?

FENWICK. Do I mean John?

ISABEL. I'm going to Cambridge next year. (*Pause.*) And then I'm going to be an archaeologist.

FENWICK. That firm tone of voice sounds rather insecure, y'know.

ISABEL. How do you expect me to sound at seventeen?

Pause.

FENWICK. Your mother was an implacably frivolous woman. She once referred to Hitler as being 'a tedious little man'. (*Drinks.*) She was addicted to such expressions. (*Drinks.*)

When she was pregnant with you it was 'tiresome'. When the
Germans went into the Sudetenland it was 'dreary'. (*Pause.*)
You look so painfully like her that I half expect you to come
out with similar idiocies. (*Drinks.*) Most unfair.

ISABEL. Poor mother!

FENWICK. She redeemed herself a little when she was dying
though.

ISABEL. How?

FENWICK. She described the prospect of eternal life as: 'just
too damned prosaic for words, darling'. (*Pause.*) Closed her
eyes, farted — and died.

ISABEL. Daddy!

FENWICK. Don't be reproachful. I adored her. I have the
greatest respect for boredom and malicious apathy. (*Pause.*)
She loathed her family, despised her class and squandered her
income. Could anything be more endearing than that?
(*Drinks.*) It's the nearest an aristocratic Englishwoman could
get to a sense of style.

ISABEL. Well I'm not frivolous. (*Pause.*) Not terribly.

FENWICK. I can't think of a better word to describe the pursuit
of archaeology. (*Refilling glass.*) Digging holes? Glueing shards?

ISABEL. You have a stupid idea of the subject.

FENWICK. No doubt a frivolous one. (*Drinks.*) Any particular
ruins in mind?

ISABEL. Are you a bit rattled?

FENWICK. I don't know. (*Pause.*) When I'm talking I never know
how I'm feeling. (*Drinks.*) Do you find that? Can't concentrate
on both at the same time.

ISABEL. I think you're evading the subject of John.

FENWICK. Am I? I'd have said I was refusing to air my
prejudices.

Pause.

ISABEL. About his being a miner's son?

FENWICK. Don't be ridiculous. It's that damned Victoria Cross.
(*Drinks.*) I can't stand bravery. What I mean is: I think bravery
is a notion that confers honour whilst being devoid of

meaning. (*Drinks.*) I regard a man who's won the Victoria
Cross as a threat to my distaste for heroism. (*Pause.*) I suppose
he's extremely modest about it.

ISABEL. He never mentions it.

FENWICK. Can you see the devilish logic there? He gets himself
blown to pieces rescuing three men and God knows what
besides. The King pins a VC on him. Then convention requires
him to disavow the idea that he's done anything unusual.
(*Pause.*) Isn't that the teeniest bit anglo-saxon?

Pause.

ISABEL. What about you and Tito's partisans, then?

FENWICK. For them it's more than a war. It's a revolution. They
regard British intelligence officers as light comedians. I
couldn't have seemed more bizarre to them if I'd worn a baggy
suit, a bowler hat and a false nose. (*Drinks.*) You ask Evelyn
and Randolph. (*Pause.*) Isabel, do I have to meet him?

JOHN *enters diffidently.* FENWICK *eyes him over the rim of
his glass.*

ISABEL. Daddy — John Baildon. (*They shake hands.*)

FENWICK. I hope you aren't dining here, you two. The food's
filthy even by wartime standards. It's my brother-in-law. He's
an introverted sort of chap. But takes refuge in playing his
idea of a foreigner's idea of an Englishman.

ISABEL. My father does tend to go on about England and the
English.

FENWICK. Yes I do it's true. I'm a francophile by inclination.
It isn't that I like the French either, but I do stand in awe
of their cuisine. (*Pause.*) Do give him a drink, Isabel. (*As she
goes to do so.*) I hope you like bourbon. Percy keeps his
booze locked up. He thinks I'm wicked, unpatriotic and
cosmopolitan. (*Drinks.*) The fact is that those were precisely
the intriguing qualities of his sister, whom I was fortunate
enough to marry. (*Reflectively.*) And who is unfortunately
doing something prosaic at the moment. (*He goes close to
JOHN, staring.*) A lot of lords do keep their booze locked up,
you know.

JOHN *returns the stare, undaunted.* ISABEL *gives him his
drink.*

JOHN. I've never had bourbon I don't think.

ISABEL. Where did you get it?

FENWICK. A present. From a chap called Djilas. He pinched it from the Kremlin. (*Pause.*) Do you find history poignant, Baildon? (*He crosses to the drinks, picks up the bourbon.*)

JOHN. Well, I —

FENWICK. One wonders how this bottle got to the Kremlin in the first place.

JOHN. I don't know much about it —

FENWICK. Oh quite. I'm sure Roosevelt doesn't keep you informed of his every move.

JOHN. I meant —

FENWICK. Only teasing, m'dear fellow.

Pause.

JOHN. I think —

Pause.

FENWICK. You do?

ISABEL. Stop it, father!

FENWICK. When Isabel switches from 'daddy' to 'father' it means I have to watch my p's and q's. How do you like Percy's castle? He says the RAF'll be the death of him. (*Drinks.*) They piss over the battlements.

JOHN *has wandered over to the radiogram. The Mozart has stopped.*

JOHN. Was that Mozart?

FENWICK. How d'you like my daughter?

JOHN. I —

FENWICK. People do piss a lot around Percy. When Isabel was a small girl she once pissed on one of his dogs. (*Drinks.*) Teatime, it was. She was riding round on this damn great labrador. My wife uttered the word 'fuck' a propos something or other. Percy dropped his teacupful of whiskey and Isabel pissed on the hound. (*Drinks.*) Mark my words, you'll be hearing the word 'fuck' on the wireless before this century's out.

Pause.

JOHN. Was it a word your wife felt strongly about?

FENWICK. She felt the sequence of events would have been of riveting interest to a Freudian. What do you think, Baildon?

ISABEL. He's drunk.

FENWICK. Plastered. Is he shocked? Are you shocked?

JOHN. It's not the kind of language I'd use in front of my own daughter.

FENWICK. You pompous little bugger. (*Drinks.*) I think I'll dine with the RAF tonight, Isabel.

ISABEL. What a jolly good idea! I didn't ask him up here for a vetting.

FENWICK. Pert, isn't she? (*Drinks.*) Pert. (*Drinks.*) Are they like that in Leeds?

Pause.

JOHN. Castleford.

FENWICK. Never heard of Castleford. Percy'd know. He practically owns the London Midland and Scottish railway. I wonder if his trains go through Castleford?

Pause.

JOHN. You'd have to change at Wakefield.

Pause.

FENWICK. You have a strange effect on me, Baildon. You stimulate conditioned reflexes I thought I'd overcome. I hope you won't take offence. I've no doubt you and yours will throw Churchill out at the next election. Then you can set chaps like Percy and me to some good honest work at last. (*Drinks.*) Making tumbrils, for instance?

JOHN. I think you're rather jumping to conclusions about me.

FENWICK. Swear cross your heart and hope to die, you won't have me shot? (*Pause.*) Then you can have Isabel. (*Drinks.*) Her mother had a navvy once. When we lived in St. Tropez. She only gave him up because she decided it was an extremely conventional way to behave. (*Drinks.*) I think we ought to have him posted to Greece, don't you Isabel? According to Djilas, Stalin's thrown Greece to the British and the

communists there'll fight like hell. (*Pause.*) And of course
there's always the Japanese.

Pause.

JOHN. I'm beginning to think this sequence of events would be
of riveting interest to a Freudian. (*Drinks.*) What do you
think Brigadier?

FENWICK. My dear Baildon. It's a rule of this house — this
castle, I should say — that the women are free to do as they
like. They've been doing it for three centuries. And even old
Percy — backward as he is — has never ruled out incest as
the best way of keeping things in the family. (*Pause.*) Isabel
and I have never been to bed, old man. But we do have a
rapport light years away from those places served by the
London Midland and Scottish. (*Drinks.*) Thwart me at your
peril. And if it's a question of that dour little stinker Attlee
for prime minister, I shall decamp to Rhodesia and organise
a rebel army over there.

*He makes an unsteady exit. ISABEL is convulsed with
laughter.*

JOHN. Is he always like that?

ISABEL. I haven't seen him for two years.

Pause.

JOHN. It's good to see you, Isabel.

ISABEL. You mustn't mind him.

JOHN. I mind him very much. (*Pause.*) I have a feeling he's quite
sober.

ISABEL. He was always a bit weird.

Pause.

JOHN. Who's Djilas?

ISABEL. I've no idea.

JOHN. Well. Can I have some more of his historical bourbon?

ISABEL (*getting it*). Are you feeling shaky?

JOHN. Does he think we're getting engaged?

Pause.

ISABEL. What do you think?

JOHN. Do I have to meet your Uncle Percy as well?

ISABEL. He's in Washington.

JOHN. I thought he was practically gaga.

ISABEL. Actually, we're all in two minds about that. (*Pause.*)
Churchill thinks the Americans think Uncle Percy's a wily
negotiator.

Pause.

JOHN. Negotiating what?

ISABEL. I believe the idea is that one throws Uncle Percy in at
the deep end without telling him anything. (*Pause.*)
Naturally nobody tells me anything of any consequence either.

JOHN. So how do you know about Churchill?

ISABEL. I read to Uncle Percy after dinner when he's had a lot
of port. (*Pause.*) He rambles.

Pause.

JOHN. What do you read?

ISABEL. Catullus, lately.

JOHN. In Latin?

ISABEL (*standing to declaim*). Odi et amo: quare id faciam,
fortasse requiris, /Nescio, sed fieri sentio et excrucior.
(*Crossing to him.*) I hate and love. You may ask why I do so.
I do not know, but I feel it and I am in torment. (*She kisses
him lightly and moves away.*)

Pause.

JOHN. This can't be how we won the war.

ISABEL. It's Uncle Percy's theory that the entire strategy was
worked out in the Vatican.

Pause.

JOHN. What?

ISABEL. He's very anti-Papist.

Pause.

JOHN. Isabel. Have you the faintest idea what you're talking
about?

ISABEL. No. How could I have? (*Pause.*) Would you say you had a coherent picture of things yourself?

JOHN. Down there in Castleford, you mean?

ISABEL. Don't you start! (*Pause.*) Daddy isn't a snob, you know. He's an ironist.

Pause.

JOHN. Don't you think he rather supports Uncle Percy's view of what foreigners are supposed to think you're all like?

ISABEL. You're not a foreigner.

Pause.

JOHN. I'm beginning to wonder.

ISABEL. Uncle Percy's not so screwy. He's merely of the opinion that Pious the Twelfth would have preferred the Nazis to the Bolsheviks.

JOHN. That should make him popular in Washington.

ISABEL. His money's on the Bolsheviks every time, he says.

JOHN. Ah yes. His money. (*Pause.*) His dividends from the London Midland and Scottish railway?

ISABEL. Mrs Roosevelt adores Uncle Percy.

JOHN. How does she feel about the Bolsheviks?

Pause.

ISABEL. With my kind of upbringing, there are no criteria for judging who's a fantasist and who isn't.

JOHN. There was nothing unreal about the mortar-bomb that landed in my jeep.

Pause.

ISABEL. I know a pub where they give you a wizard blackmarket dinner. (*Pause: he is listening to something outside the window.*) John?

We hear a chorus of RAF voices singing: 'We're three little lambs, who have lost our way' etc.
    ISABEL *and* JOHN *listen for a moment.*

ISABEL. Isn't it moving?

Scene Three

MRS BAILDON's *kitchen/living-room. Some weeks later. She is pouring hot water into a teapot.*

FENWICK — *in the uniform of a brigadier, and a greatcoat — stands with his back to her looking out of the window.*

FENWICK. It's a bleak day. (*Pause.*) We had a nasty skid coming out of Wakefield. (*Pause.*) The street decorations brighten things up.

MRS BAILDON. Them flags? Aye. It's all for VE Day tomorrow. I've a cake in the oven for t'bairns' teaparty. And I've no doubt their fathers'll be suppin' theirsens daft all night afterwards. (*Pause.*) Won't you take your top coat off, sir?

Pause.

FENWICK. Not 'sir'. Please, Mrs Baildon. (*He takes his coat off.*)

MRS BAILDON. I will say, it didn't come natural to me. It's thirty years sin' I were in service.

FENWICK. At least the war's broken down some of the old prejudices, don't you think?

MRS BAILDON. Has it?

FENWICK. I've always found that sort of thing rather ugly.

She brings the teapot to the table, and takes cups and saucers from a cupboard.

MRS BAILDON. I went out to be a scullery maid when I were thirteen. There's a photo of me somewhere, wi' a little tin trunk and a right mad expression. (*Pause.*) I were naught but a skivvy, really. In one of them private schools for young gentlemen. (*Pause.*) I got t'sack for chucking a gravy-boat at one on 'em. (*Smiles.*) He pinched my bottom when I were serving. (*Pause.*) One road or another, it could have been you Mr Fenwick.

FENWICK. I should hope not!

MRS BAILDON. Aye. Well that place were no Eton, I can tell you.

Pause.

FENWICK. Harrow. In my case.

MRS BAILDON. Half on 'em were no' but jumped up farmers' sons. (*Pause.*) Won't you sit down?

He sits down in her husband's old chair. She gives him his tea at the table with her own. They size each other up.

MRS BAILDON. I'm sure I don't know what to make on it all.

Pause.

FENWICK. I didn't quite know what to make of your letter, either.

MRS BAILDON. I hope you didn't think me impertinent.

Pause.

FENWICK. I think it was a very good idea for us to meet. But I don't know whether we shall see eye to eye.

MRS BAILDON. I wasn't counting on that.

There is a green plush cover on the mantelpiece with a clock, various knick-knacks, and a beautifully clean and polished miner's lamp. FENWICK *looks at it.*

FENWICK. Was that your husband's lamp?

MRS BAILDON. Nay. He had his with him. (*Pause.*) They didn't get them out, you see. (*Pause.*) That on the shelf was my father's. (*Pause.*) John got it out and cleaned it up when he were a little lad. (*Pause.*) But they not exactly ornaments, are they? I've never liked it there.

Pause.

FENWICK. So you want me to put a stop to this friendship between Isabel and John?

MRS BAILDON. I do an' all.

Pause.

FENWICK. We've all been through the war together. I think there's a new democratic spirit in this country. (*Sips his tea.*) And about time too.

MRS BAILDON. That's right. And summat tells me our John's up to no democratic good wi' your daughter.

Pause.

FENWICK. I couldn't possibly intervene.

MRS BAILDON. Why not? By all accounts you and John got off on t'wrong foot from the start. He wrote and told me so from Germany. (*Pause.*) He rarely says owt to me face. What he does, he hints at things in his letters.

Pause.

FENWICK. I disliked him on sight. (*Pause.*) It was all most unfortunate.

MRS BAILDON. Did you dislike him? Or what he is and where he comes from? —

FENWICK. I'm not a snob, Mrs Baildon.

Pause.

MRS BAILDON. I am.

Pause.

FENWICK. Could you clarify that a little?

Pause.

MRS BAILDON. Your wife ran wi' a funny set didn't she? Afore t'war?

Pause.

FENWICK (*smiling*). Are you reproaching me with scandals in the family, Mrs Baildon?

MRS BAILDON. Nay. I were wondering how your Isabel were brought up.

FENWICK. Now that is just a little impertinent.

MRS BAILDON. Happen so.

Pause.

FENWICK. Come now. (*Pause.*) My wife was an alcoholic, a depressive, and in every way an unhappy woman. (*He lights a cigarette.*) I don't suppose the working class has a monopoly of misery.

MRS BAILDON. She made a right splash on her misery. Her face were never out o' t'papers, afore the war.

FENWICK. That's quite enough, Mrs Baildon.

MRS BAILDON. You're not talking to one on your servants.

Pause.

FENWICK. My brother-in-law Percy's, actually. Five are in the army, two of them seriously wounded. Three in the Waafs, one in the Wrens, two on the land. (*Pause.*) And one conscientious objector felling trees in Wales.

Pause.

MRS BAILDON. But I recognised the tone of voice, Mr Fenwick.

Pause.

FENWICK. Then I beg your pardon.

Pause.

MRS BAILDON. I give short shrift to scandal meself.

FENWICK. I'm delighted to hear it.

MRS BAILDON. Anyroad. You're mucking along all right, are you?

FENWICK. I'm sorry?

MRS BAILDON. Wi'out servants.

Pause.

FENWICK. Did you share your husband's political convictions?

MRS BAILDON. I don't know as working men's wives ever do.

Pause.

FENWICK. Quite.

Pause. She gestures at the room.

MRS BAILDON. I shared this wi' him. (*Pause.*) And never knowing from one day to t'next whether he'd come back from yon pit. (*Pause.*) Then one day he didn't.

FENWICK. I'm so sorry.

Pause.

MRS BAILDON. I remember some photos of Lady Dorothy. In Picture Post. (*Pause.*) Did you go with her to them Olympic Games in Berlin? Supping and dancin' wi' Nazis? (*Pause.*) According to my husband, folk in this country didn't know the half of it.

Pause.

FENWICK. This is shameful, Mrs Baildon.

MRS BAILDON. I am? Or what I'm talking about?

Pause.

FENWICK. I suppose there's no reason why you should know I fought in the Spanish Civil War.

MRS BAILDON. Who for? Franco?

Pause.

FENWICK. For the Republic. (*Pause.*) The . . . (*Grins.*) . . .
the toffs were there as well, you know.

MRS BAILDON. What did your wife make on that, I wonder?

Pause.

FENWICK. In nineteen thirty-six we lost a boy in the battle of
Madrid. He was in a British machine-gun section with a
battalion of Germans. (*Pause.*) He ran away from Oxford in his
first term. He was eighteen. Ten years older than Isabel.
(*Pause.*) My wife was indeed on one of her many sporting
visits to Germany. No doubt swilling champagne with some of
those who later on were swilling it with Russians, over the
Nazi-Soviet pact. (*Pause.*) What did your husband make of
that, by the way? (*Pause.*) However I went to Spain to try and
persuade Douglas to come back. (*Pause.*) He was dead when
I got there. (*Pause.*) I stayed. (*Pause.*) Have you got anything
stronger than tea, I wonder?

*They stare at each other. She goes to a cupboard and gets a
bottle of whiskey and a glass. She sets the glass in front of
him and pours a stiff drink.*

MRS BAILDON. Our Brian's. Black market. (*Pause.*) Why not?
he says. I practically own yon pub.

Pause. FENWICK *sips his whiskey.*

FENWICK. I can assure you, Mrs Baildon. I believe in
absolutely nothing at all.

Pause.

MRS BAILDON. You and my son's wearing the same uniform.

FENWICK. You must be proud of his Victoria Cross.

MRS BAILDON. I'd sooner he'd come through it wi'out a mark
on him.

FENWICK. But a local hero though, surely?

MRS BAILDON (*shouting*). I've never mentioned his damned
Victoria Cross! (*Crosses to the table and strikes it with her
fist.*) They gi' nowt to his father!

Pause.

FENWICK. As a matter of fact. I was told my wife once poured a glass of champagne down Goering's neck. (*Pause.*) The story goes that she then refilled it and shouted: here's to the German battalion of the International Brigade! (*Pause.*) Scandals do tend to be so one-sided, don't you think?

He refills his glass and drains it. Adds a little more. She goes back to the fire. Stands with her back to him.

MRS BAILDON. I don't want my son wi' your daughter.

Pause.

FENWICK. Isabel went down by train to meet him back from Germany this morning. (*Pause.*) I'm only going to London because I have a conference at the War Office tonight. (*Drinks.*) Coming between young lovers isn't quite my style, Mrs Baildon. (*Refills his glass.*)

MRS BAILDON. What is your style then? The girl's no' but seventeen.

Pause.

FENWICK. Her mother's mental age . . . at that age . . . I'd have put somewhere in the mid-forties. (*Drinks.*) Isabel takes after her. (*Drinks.*) What's my style? I'm a bit of an alcoholic too. (*Pause.*) I used to drink with Dorothy. (*Pause.*) For Dorothy, I should say. (*Drinks.*) Her battle slogan was: phenomena are squalid. (*Drinks.*) Her drinking slogan, I should say. Her drinking style, d'you see? (*Pause.*) She had style. She was an enchanting woman who was absolutely dismayed by the failure of the upper classes to be anything but philistine. (*Drinks.*) As she put it. (*Pause.*) So she affected either languor or savagery according to her mood — and an otherwise highly original personality was drowned in a sea of despair. (*Pause.*) Things like the 'Twenty-six Strike got on her nerves awfully. Said she wanted a real revolution. Didn't give a damn which end of the political spectrum it came from, so long as it was — fun! (*Pause.*) I'm extremely tired, Mrs Baildon. I've spent the last two years on a most exhausting mission abroad, for which I had neither the wit nor the flexibility. My fluency in Serbo-Croat got me into it. That's what comes of making Slavonic studies one's speciality.

MRS BAILDON. I'm right sorry for you Mr Fenwick!

FENWICK. What the devil do you want me to do?

MRS BAILDON. It's not for me to say.

He goes to the window and stands looking out.

FENWICK. My driver's looking pretty sullen.

MRS BAILDON. Ask him in for a cup of tea.

He turns to stare at her, and turns back to the window. She grins. She pours another drink and goes up to him, touches his shoulder lightly.

MRS BAILDON. Here —

FENWICK. I'm not going to be very popular with your Brian.

MRS BAILDON. It's funny isn't it?

FENWICK. What is?

MRS BAILDON. When there's no servants' hall to send your man for his cup of tea.

Pause.

FENWICK. Mrs Baildon you exasperate me!

Pause.

MRS BAILDON. You're the one that thinks there ought to be nothing standing between us. (*Pause.*) There is, though. (*Pause.*) I can't judge your daughter because I don't know her. (*Pause.*) But our John? (*Pause.*) I've stood over him with his books at that table night after night. Year after year. (*Pause.*) His father and brother and me went without to put a school uniform on his back. To find him cricket clothes and a lot besides. To keep up wi' the others at yon grammar school. (*Pause.*) My son's taken the sacrifices of them that's round him, Mr Fenwick. And he's got to understand what he owes. (*Pause.*) I can't put it plainer.

FENWICK. I see. (*Pause.*) John's something of an investment, is he?

MRS BAILDON. Since when was investment a dirty word to somebody like you?

FENWICK. Touché!

MRS BAILDON. Whatever that means.

FENWICK (*finishing his drink*). I'll be off.

He puts on his greatcoat. Finds his cap.

FENWICK. I won't insult either John or Isabel by pretending
to read the paternal riot act. It wouldn't convince me, never
mind them. (*Pause.*) It's true Isabel is precocious and wilful.
Agnostic in all things. A wild one. (*Pause.*) As I said, her
mother's child. (*Pause.*) It's also true she was designed by
birth and all the traditional hocus-pocus for a life of horses,
empty social ritual and young men of daunting imbecility.
But it seems she's immune, thank God. (*Pause.*) Granted
wartime is hardly the setting for the vacuous manners and
idiotic pursuits of the thirties. All the same, I feel she'd have
rejected that nonsense anyway. (*Pause.*) I love her very much,
Mrs Baildon. I respect her. Above all I admire her originality,
her right to those solemn freedoms to which the young are
sometimes properly dedicated. (*Pause.*) She'll not concede
that your son has no place in her future, or she in his. She'll
simply not grasp it. (*Pause.*) If I find out where they are in
London, I intend to send them champagne. (*Pause.*) It's
been fascinating to meet you. (*At the door.*) Is it a question
of lacking a common language? (*Pause.*) I'm damned sure
it isn't class. (*Pause.*) Good day to you —

He touches his cap and goes out. MRS BAILDON *goes to her
husband's old chair. She runs her hands over the cracked
leather, tugs at a protruding tuft of horsehair. She goes to the
window. We hear* FENWICK's *car driving away. She takes
the miner's lamp off the mantelpiece, stands looking at it a
moment, then puts it away in a drawer. She sits looking into the
fire.*

Scene Four

*A hotel bedroom in London. Early evening the next day. An
ice-bucket with two bottles of champagne. A portable
gramophone with records in the lid of the case.*
ISABEL *lies on the rumpled bed in her dressing-gown.*
JOHN, *in shirt and trousers, is about to open one of the
bottles. The cork pops. He pours two glasses and holds them up.*

JOHN. Courtesy of Brigadier Fenwick.

ISABEL. Whose spies are everywhere.

He takes the champagne to the bed. They touch glasses.

JOHN. Here's to you —

ISABEL. Here's to you

They drink. He touches her glass with his again.

JOHN. To us?

Pause.

ISABEL. I'm superstitious.

They look at each other. He goes to the window. We hear the sound of a crowd outside, singing 'Roll Out the Barrel'. It fades in the distance. JOHN *closes the window and raises his glass.*

JOHN. To VE Day. (*Pause.*) To victory in Europe?

ISABEL (*mock solemnity*). Victory in Europe.

They drink. He goes to the bed.

JOHN. I want you again, Isabel.

ISABEL. Just now was the fourth time since lunch. You're nothing but a walking erection, that's what you are.

Pause.

JOHN. Shall we go out?

ISABEL. Open the window again.

He goes to the window. Opens it and leans out. Singing, laughter, the sound of crowds in the street.
ISABEL *goes to the dressing table. Sits down and begins to brush her hair.*

ISABEL. I think it's the first time — illness apart — that I've spent a whole day in bed.

He crosses to stand behind her, looking at her reflection in the mirror.

JOHN. You weren't a virgin, you bitch!

ISABEL. Wasn't I?

Pause.

JOHN. Well?

ISABEL. Well what?

JOHN. Who and when?

ISABEL. A divine squadron leader. Last summer.

She turns to look at him. He hits her across the face so hard that she nearly falls off the stool. He goes to fill his champagne glass. Holds up the bottle.

JOHN. I rather liked your father. (*Pause.*) I'd like to be like him. (*Pause.*) In some ways.

ISABEL *examines her cheek in the mirror.*

ISABEL (*turning*). Are you suffering from post-coital depression?

Pause.

JOHN. That insulting way he has of turning a phrase. (*Pause.*) I think he's unsure of himself, though. (*Pause.*) He's not exactly a man of conviction.

ISABEL. He's never been short of convictions. You can convince him of practically anything.

JOHN. I do admire his nasty social manner.

ISABEL (*brushing*). Some girls don't have a hymen at all, you know.

JOHN. You were a virgin?

ISABEL. Yes I was a bloody virgin!

Pause.

JOHN. Still. (*Pause.*) I enjoyed hitting you. (*Pause.*) Have some more champagne.

She holds out her glass and he refills it.

ISABEL. My mother said that sex is the only experience that can't be overrated.

JOHN. How old were you when she died?

ISABEL. Eleven.

JOHN. What a disgusting way to speak to your eleven-year-old daughter.

ISABEL. She didn't say it to me. She was repulsing an attaché.

JOHN. In her boudoir?

ISABEL. In a deckchair on the Queen Mary.

JOHN. What was he using? Grappling irons?

Pause.

ISABEL. Sex can't be overrated, she said — because a sensible woman approaches it with minimal expectations.

Pause.

JOHN. And little Isabel was eavesdropping nearby, and bouncing her ball?

ISABEL. I certainly wasn't bouncing the attaché's.

Pause.

JOHN. No doubt that was your mother's prerogative.

ISABEL. I think if you try hard, you might actually get to sound like my father.

JOHN. Shall we go and dance in the streets with the hoi polloi?

ISABEL. Were you a virgin?

Pause.

JOHN. Shall we go and dance in the streets with the hoi polloi?

ISABEL. I thought you were the Cary Grant of Castleford Grammar —

JOHN. Ossett. (*Pause.*) Castleford don't sport a grammar school, m'dear.

ISABEL. Ossett. (*Pause.*) Ossett! (*Pause.*) Ossett? (*Pause.*) Gosh!

JOHN *lights a cigarette and stretches out on the bed.*

JOHN. You can have a girl in Germany for a packet of fags.

ISABEL. Well that puts me in my place.

JOHN. What does?

ISABEL. You had me for nothing.

She swings round to face him. He tosses his cigarette packet into her lap. She stares at it a long moment.

ISABEL. Little frauleins.

Pause.

JOHN. That's right. (*Pause.*) And occupation clap.

Pause.

ISABEL. Did you?

Pause.

JOHN. No. (*Pause.*) There's a skinny little kid of twelve who regards me as a father-figure. And that's about my limit.

ISABEL. A little girl?

JOHN. I found her living in a burnt-out tank. (*Pause.*) Her father's dead. Her mother's in Russia somewhere. (*Pause.*) No other family. (*Pause.*) I shall do my damndest to get her to England.

ISABEL. Why that particular one?

Pause.

JOHN. You have to pick on somebody.

Pause.

ISABEL. It's gone very quiet. What's happened to the sweaty masses?

JOHN (*crossing to window*). I can't see a sweaty mass. Not a single one.

ISABEL. You're a sweaty mass. You're a jerk. (*She begins to dress.*) How did you get back from Germany so quickly?

JOHN. Thumbed a lift in a dying Lancaster.

ISABEL. From where?

JOHN. Near a place called Belsen.

ISABEL. I thought you said you were bringing a portable gramophone?

JOHN. It's over there.

ISABEL. Well put a record on then.

He crosses to the gramophone. Opens the case. Takes out two or three records from the lid.

JOHN. My God! (*At the records.*) Not quite us, I wouldn't say.

ISABEL *crosses to the bed. Stands looking at it. She kicks it.*

ISABEL. You did some pretty amazing things to me in this bed today.

JOHN. They also serve, who only kneel and push.

ISABEL. Don't be revolting.

JOHN. I'm coarse-natured. But struggling for refinement.

ISABEL. It was divine.

Pause.

JOHN. Isabel —

ISABEL. What?

JOHN. You do tend to use that word a bit, you know. Don't you think it verges on hyperbole?

ISABEL. I think in the context that's an insulting thing to say. (*Pause.*) It was extremely divine. Quite definitely smashing. A revelation. (*Pause.*) For one thing, I'd never stopped to consider that two people add up to such a fantastic number of holes. (*Pause.*) John Player and Sons must be proud of you.

JOHN. Isabel I promise you I did nothing like that in Germany.

ISABEL. D'you mean like what we did? Or for cigarettes?

JOHN. Neither.

Pause.

ISABEL. Then the thought crosses my mind that sexually speaking, you're ahead of your time.

He has been winding the gramophone. Stops. Goes to her.

JOHN. Oh yes? (*Pause.*) I went out with a girl in Wakefield for three years before she let me inside her blouse. Can you imagine? (*Pause.*) We used to walk in the park of a Sunday afternoon. Every Sunday afternoon for three years. I once worked it out. Say three hours a Sunday, that's three times three times fifty-two. I make that four hundred and sixty-eight hours of doomed erection-time.

Pause.

ISABEL. And then?

JOHN. And then she wouldn't let me unfasten her brassière.

ISABEL. Why not?

JOHN. We weren't engaged.

A woman's voice outside singing 'Land of Hope and Glory'. ISABEL goes to the window.

ISABEL. It's a woman hanging out of the window opposite. She's waving a gin bottle in one hand and a Union Jack in the other.

Others in the street amiably join in. The sound swells to an impressive crescendo. JOHN listens, immobile. After a moment he springs across the room and shuts the window.

ISABEL. Spoilsport!

Pause. He sits on the bed.

JOHN. It's all a bit premature. Isn't it?

ISABEL sits at the dressing-table and begins to make up.

ISABEL. It's like a great big party. (*Pause.*) All over London. (*Pause.*) The whole country. (*Pause.*) I think they've got a right to shout and sing and get drunk if they want to.

Pause.

JOHN. Nay. So do I.

ISABEL. Well then.

Pause.

JOHN. That's right. (*Pause.*) No more blackout. Sirens. Bombs. (*Pause.*) Rationing. (*Pause.*) No more bloody Tories!

ISABEL. Personally, I consider politics a huge bore.

JOHN. The men that's coming back, they won't stand anything like the nineteen thirties again. (*Pause.*) They won't have it.

ISABEL. Well. I'm going to school in Switzerland for a year. And then I'm going to Cambridge. (*Pause.*) You'll be demobbed. You'll go to medical school. And in about a hundred years you'll become a famous surgeon. (*Pause.*) So —

JOHN. I thought we were supposed to be in love, Isabel.

Pause.

ISABEL. I thought we were having an affaire. With an 'e'. Like the French. (*Pause.*) Something beautiful and not frightfully serious.

Pause.

JOHN. The thought crosses my mind that morally speaking, you're ahead of my time!

Pause.

ISABEL. I thought it was love too.

JOHN. Till when?

ISABEL. Till today. (*Pause.*) Till just now.

JOHN. And now?

Pause.

ISABEL. I think I'm rather taken by lust. (*Pause.*) Very taken by lust. (*Pause.*) It's exhilarating. It definitely puts men in perspective. In their true perspective, one might say.

JOHN. You're getting back at me because I hit you.

ISABEL. No. (*Pause.*) That was thrilling.

JOHN. Can't you ever find a middle way between bravado and affectation?

ISABEL. I'm sure I shall grow out of it. (*Pause.*) Anyway, what's wrong with lust?

JOHN. I don't think it has a future.

ISABEL. It's vulgar to think about the future.

JOHN. As mummy used to say?

ISABEL. No. She thought it was middle-class to think about the future. (*Pause.*) You needn't adopt a sneering tone about her. She was a free spirit. Our lot weren't all stuffed shirts and waxwork flappers, you know.

Pause.

JOHN. Our lot. (*Pause.*) That says it all.

ISABEL. I can't argue with a bigot.

JOHN. Let alone marry one.

ISABEL. At my age?

JOHN. What age would you consider suitable?

Pause.

ISABEL. Never.

JOHN. I'd say that's a ridiculous point of view at your age. Are you against it with me? Or in principle?

ISABEL. Both.

JOHN. You liked me well enough in bed.

ISABEL. I should think there's hundreds of men I'd like well enough in bed. (*Pause.*) As to the principle. I think marriage is just one of those things that'll have to go, sooner or later. (*She looks at him, then rushes to him and flings her arms round his neck.*) Oh he's a beautiful scrubbed handsome bewildered young officer!

He grabs her by the throat, forces her onto the bed and half throttles her. She faints in his grip. He kneels back on the bed looking down at her. Very distantly from outside: laughter, short bursts of singing.
He goes out and returns with a glass of water which he throws over her face. She groans and stirs. He pours the remainder of the champagne into their glasses. ISABEL sits up, feeling at her throat.

JOHN. Have some more champagne.

He puts her glass by the bedside. She mops at her face with the sheet. He moves away and finds his own glass.

I think you've misunderstood me. Or shall I say you've misunderstood the way I look at things. (*Pause.*) The way I look at them is. (*Drinks.*) Let me put it this way. A diffident working-class child with a fantastically ambitious mother slogs his way through grammar school. Whilst his father studies the Bolshevik Revolution between shifts at the pit. (*Pause.*) Our dutiful hero wins a scholarship to medical school, a Victoria Cross under mortar fire, three pips on his shoulder and a peer's niece at a boozy party on the night of the investiture. (*Drinks.*) So far so good. (*Pause.*) He fiddles a week's leave from Germany to be with the posh bint on VE night. (*Crosses to the dressing-table, absently regards his reflection in the mirror.*) He . . . er . . . has her. Drinks her eccentric father's champagne. Proposes. (*Pause.*) And having half throttled her in revulsion at an ill-timed gesture of reconciliation . . . however insincere . . . can only stare at the image in this mirror in frank disbelief. (*Pause.*) It's a success story in its way. But — as your mother might very well have said, I imagine — somehow darling it isn't me. (*He drains his glass.*) None of it.

ISABEL *reaches for her glass and sips with difficulty.*

ISABEL. What would be you, darling?

He sits at the dressing-table, looking into the mirror.

JOHN. We're setting up displaced persons' camps in Germany. (*Pause.*) Death camp survivors. Jews. Gypsies. Liberated prisoners of war. Deserters. Orphans. (*Pause.*) Not to mention quite a few Nazis on the run, trying to hide among their own victims. (*Pause.*) And Russians. (*Pause.*) How I wish my father could have met and talked to some of those Russians!

Pause.

ISABEL. What would be you, darling?

Pause.

JOHN. Without wishing to exaggerate. I feel a bit of a displaced person myself. (*Pause.*) One Russian infantryman told me he wanted to come to England. An anglophile, he said. He'd been a prisoner of war, which meant as likely as not he'd be treated as a deserter in the Soviet Union. (*Pause.*) Why England? I asked him. (*Pause.*) He rather fancied himself as a wit. We're told you're a nation of class-ridden muddlers, he said. I'd prefer that to either the American dream or the Soviet nightmare (*Pause.*) He died of typhus, or he'd have been handed back to the Red Army. (*Pause.*) He also died laughing, since I was trying to explain at the time where the Bolshevik Revolution had gone wrong. (*Holds the bottle over his glass — it is empty.*) One blushes, darling. One simply blushes, at the recollection.

He lifts out the other bottle of champagne. The ice has turned to water and it is dripping. He opens it. She is watching all the time. He fills their glasses and goes back to the dressing-table.

JOHN (*sits, raises his glass*). I am Semyon Vassilievitch Rusakov. I believe in democracy, dogs and decency. (*Drinks.*) Proletariat fit to vote but not to rule. Which is advance on Soviet Union, where they are considered fit for neither. (*Turns, bows to her, drinks.*) Cheers, John Baildonovitch! Typhus at least knows no frontiers.

ISABEL. Don't be maudlin, sweetheart.

JOHN. That's right. Let's be lascivious instead.

ISABEL. One shudders to think.

JOHN. Ah yes. But what?

ISABEL. That if the new Education Act's anything to go by, the grammar schools'll be turning out people like you by the thousand in a few years' time. (*Drinks.*) Ugh! What a prospect!

Pause. He goes to her.

JOHN. I really must have you again Isabel.

ISABEL. Do you think violence excites me?

JOHN. Does it?

Pause.

ISABEL. As long as you don't get too carried away.

Pause.

JOHN. The latest aphrodisiac. Half-hearted strangulation. (*Pause.*) Are you a bugger for punishment, as they say?

Pause.

ISABEL. I'm just not in the least bit frightened of you. That's all.

Pause.

JOHN. Shall we be lovers for ever and ever? (*Drinks.*) Shall we have a lifetime's affaire with an 'e' like the French? (*Drinks.*) I'll become a distinguished gynaecologist and do your hysterectomy in the fullness of time. (*Drinks.*) You can always rely on me. Old John. Always there in a crisis. Scalpel in hand. (*Pause.*) Shall we have an obscenely sexy passion for each other till the stars turn cold?

Pause.

ISABEL. That's more the sort of thing I had in mind.

JOHN. Till the sun burns out?

ISABEL. Till the moon falls, lover-boy!

He sits beside her on the bed. They reach for each other's hands.

JOHN. My hero is Chekhov. (*Pause.*) I regard medicine as little more than an honourable — if distasteful — way of making a living. (*Pause.*) I intend to write, Isabel. (*Drinks.*) Eventually. (*Pause.*) I shan't make a fuss about it. I shall do it. (*Pause.*) Meanwhile. Medicine for mother, and art in secret for John. How about that? (*Pause.*) How's about that?

Pause.

ISABEL. I am feeling quite randy again, as a matter of fact.

JOHN. I think I'm a bit drunk.

ISABEL. Me too. (*Pause.*) Let's see what it's like drunk.

JOHN. Wow!

Pause.

ISABEL. Medicine for mother. Art for John. And sex for Isabel. (*Pause.*) Yum-yum.

Pause.

JOHN. I shall never tell anyone else about the writing, Isabel. Only you.

ISABEL. A wise precaution. You should never disregard an intuition that you're attempting the impossible.

He stares hard at her. She smiles cheerfully. He goes to the window a little unsteadily and peers out.

JOHN. What do you think of little old VE Day then?

Pause.

ISABEL. I think: thank God it's all over. Now we can get back
to normal. (*Pause.*) What do you think?

Pause.

JOHN. I think: by Christ things are going to be different!

*The room is nearly dark. He crosses to the gramophone,
switching a lamp on. As he kneels to put on a record:*

JOHN. Let's have one dance. Then go to bed. (*Pause.*) Then
we'll go out into London and raise hell. (*Pause.*) Okay?

Pause.

ISABEL. Okay.

*The record begins to play. Vera Lynn singing 'When the
Lights Go on Again'. JOHN fills the glasses and they move
close. They stand drinking over each other's shoulders and
swaying to the music.*

Curtain

Act Two

Scene One

The sitting-room of a house in Regents Park, London. Early evening. Time: the present.

JOHN BAILDON, now in his early fifties, sits opposite his young wife EMMA. She is reading. A Mozart horn concerto is playing. JOHN gets up and stops the record.

JOHN. That remark wasn't funny, Emma.

EMMA. No?

JOHN. It wasn't even witty.

EMMA. I don't care. What's wit? (*Pause.*) The last refuge of a cornered mind.

Pause.

JOHN. It was whimsical. And flat.

He goes to pour two drinks. Takes one to her. She goes on reading.

JOHN. You people just don't seem to have a sense of humour.

EMMA. Who?

JOHN. You know. Your political friends.

EMMA. Do I just get lumped in with them, then?

JOHN. I wish you'd known my father. He was a communist. Party member. (*Pause.*) For him the Fourth International didn't exist. It simply wasn't there. A hole in space. (*Pause.*) Such an institution might fit the bill for skaters, he thought. Or show jumpers. But for him. Speaking as an oppressed miner. It just wasn't on.

EMMA. Ha.

Pause.

JOHN. You used to have a sense of humour when I first met
you. (*Pause.*) It began to wither when you discovered the
class struggle. (*Pause.*) Once you decided you really had seen
the light, it disappeared entirely.

EMMA. I'd rather be politically mesmerised —

JOHN. Quite.

EMMA. Than morally inert.

    Pause.

JOHN. Interesting chap. Mesmer.

EMMA. Croesus more your type.

JOHN. Croesus? As in —

EMMA. As in rich as. Quite.

    Pause.

JOHN. Two years of marriage have absolutely convinced me —
Emma? — that you and I should get acquainted.

    Pause.

EMMA. I warn you John. I decided before you came in that I
wouldn't be provoked this evening. (*Pause.*) So let me read.
Will you?

    Pause.

JOHN. I was an idealist at your age. (*Pause.*) Very left, I was.
(*Pause.*) But shied away from your lot's kind of vulgar
fanaticism.

EMMA. Better than middle-aged blandness.

    Pause.

JOHN. I do wish you'd come to Haiti with me.

EMMA. My vulgar fanaticism shies away from it.

JOHN. Must be an extraordinary place.

EMMA. You do abortions. It'd be a terrific name for you.

JOHN. What would?

EMMA. Baby Doc.

    He holds up one hand, dangling from the wrist.

JOHN. His long, pale, tapering surgeon's fingers —

EMMA. What?

JOHN. The phrase stuck in my mind. From one of those romantic novels my mother used to read when I was a boy. (*Examines his nails.*) I might never have ended up in Wimpole Street if I hadn't read that book. Secretly. (*Pause.*) Flushing at the huge excitement of it all. (*Pause.*) I took some gall-stones out of a poet this morning.

EMMA. Oh yes?

JOHN. And guess what?

EMMA. They were inscribed: in the beginning was the Word?

Pause.

JOHN. The anaesthetist told me that when this poet was going under, he said: at least we had the sixties. They were our golden age. (*Pause.*) And then they wheeled him in. (*Pause.*) Amazingly large balls, he had.

EMMA. For a poet?

JOHN. I don't think I've operated on one before.

EMMA. I wonder how he got rich enough to afford you?

JOHN. Knackers the size of walnuts. (*Pause.*) The theatre sister was mesmerised by them. (*Pause.*) Good old sex.

EMMA. And good old marriage.

JOHN. Ah well. It isn't every young wife can be a revolutionary on sixty thousand a year. (*To his hand.*) His long, pale, tapering —

EMMA. I didn't marry you for that.

He stands with his empty glass. Smiles blandly.

JOHN. No, Emma. (*Amiably.*) You married me for my prick. Didn't you?

He goes for another drink.

EMMA. What did that freaky German marry you for in the fifties?

JOHN. She was not freaky. (*Pause.*) The concept was unknown in the fifties, as I recall. (*Pause.*) I wonder how she's doing over there in Argentina.

EMMA. On the run?

JOHN. My dear Emma. Gisele was a child of twelve at the end of the war. (*Pause.*) I found her living in a burnt-out tank near

Marienborn. (*Pause.*) She became almost a sort of regimental mascot. (*Pause.*) A kind of charm.

EMMA. Didn't bring you much luck!

JOHN. Such are the unhappy rewards of the status 'in loco parentis'.

EMMA. Touching though. (*Drinks.*) Salvages a little war orphan in nineteen forty-five. Marries her in fifty-five. And screws her up in three years flat.

JOHN. Wives were still very much the thing in the fifties. (*Pause.*) It's true I should have done the sensible thing and moved heaven and earth to marry Isabel after the war. But she did so yearn for digs. And tombs, and so on.

EMMA. Are you still off to Rome tomorrow?

JOHN. I am.

EMMA. I need some extra money.

JOHN. I suppose it's too much to hope these donations will buy my neck? In the unlikely event of your glum friends ever being thrust to power?

EMMA. My brother needs it. (*Pause.*) He's in Rome at the moment, oddly enough.

JOHN. He needs it for what? The final absolution?

EMMA. His dear wife thinks he has a woman there.

JOHN. How extravagant. And him an economist.

EMMA. Keep your bloody money then.

JOHN. I hate him.

EMMA. Why?

JOHN. One has to pick on somebody.

EMMA. I'd like to know why.

Pause.

JOHN. He's a monetarist. (*Pause.*) I hate monetarists.

EMMA. I don't think I know what they are.

JOHN. And you're supposed to be a Marxist? Don't you read the opposition?

EMMA. Don't be frivolous.

JOHN. Ah well. They don't believe in an opposition. Do they?

EMMA. You really are stupefyingly ignorant. Politically.

JOHN. I understand the money supply question.

EMMA. And irrelevant.

JOHN. You wouldn't think so if you knew anything about Weimar Germany in the twenties.

EMMA. Even the German freak wasn't born then.

JOHN. Do you only know about what's happened since you were born? (*Drinks.*) It squares. (*Pause.*) It all squares.

EMMA. Aren't we supposed to be going out to dinner?

JOHN. If I'd said that, you'd have accused me of being evasive.

EMMA *goes to pour herself another drink.*

EMMA. I'm tired of this endless friction.

JOHN. Friction? I thought it was almost conversation.

EMMA. You know what I mean.

Pause.

JOHN. I most certainly do.

Pause.

EMMA. I'll go up and change.

Pause.

JOHN. Let's go to bed first.

EMMA. I sometimes wonder — how you can do it when you've been operating.

JOHN. Dear Emma —

EMMA. I meant just — bodies, and so on. You know.

JOHN. They're not bodies to me. They're just an endless series of threats to my reputation.

Pause.

EMMA. Drink up, then.

Pause.

JOHN. I think I'll — have one more tiny one.

As she finds the bottle and refills his glass:

EMMA. And then. Having established that you felt like a quickie. You'll realise there isn't time before going out.

JOHN. Impertinent hussy. (*Drinks.*)

EMMA *sits. They regard each other warily.*

JOHN. I'm racked with lust.

EMMA. So what's the delay?

JOHN (*finding his cheque-book*). I don't think I could do you justice without writing your brother Robert a cheque.

EMMA. You can stuff it up your arse.

Pause.

JOHN (*putting the cheque-book away*). I thought the sixties were pretty ravy myself, as a matter of fact. (*Pause.*) You'll hardly recall them.

EMMA. Come off it. I got my first period in nineteen sixty-five.

Pause.

JOHN. That would be when you went on the pill, I suppose.

EMMA. Change the cassette, John.

JOHN. Funny that.

EMMA. What?

JOHN. People used to say: play another record. Or —

EMMA. Anyway. The sixties were just one more elaborate mystification of the working class.

JOHN. How odd. And I thought people were rather enjoying themselves at the time.

EMMA. Oh, at the time! And you see how it's turned out?

JOHN. I expect your brother'd say we were just printing money, in a way. Not fun. Banknotes. (*Pause.*) You ought to read the Financial Times, Emma. I believe Trotsky always kept a beady eye on the capitalist press. After all, he wrote for it. (*Pause.*) I read somewhere that at meetings of the Politburo he used to read Baudelaire. (*Pause.*) Any of your mob got a weakness for Baudelaire?

EMMA (*shouting*). Oh shut up!

JOHN *inclines his head over his glass in embarrassment.*

EMMA. Bugger Baudelaire!

JOHN. That's just how my father felt about Ramsay Macdonald. Couldn't stand to hear the name.

Pause.

EMMA (*quietly*). How I despise you sometimes.

JOHN. That's because you confuse my even temper with lack of feeling. (*Refilling his glass.*) I shouldn't think I'll get you upstairs in your present mood. Have another.

She thrusts out her glass and he refills it.

JOHN. Pity my parents are dead. (*Pause.*) You might have seen the inside of a working-class home for once in your life. (*Pause.*) Much more instructive than having the piss taken out of you at the factory gates with that turgid rag you try to sell them. (*He stands holding the bottle, staring vaguely ahead.*) What amuses me about your friends though is their conception of democracy. Bring your disagreements into the party, comrade. And once inside, as history taught us long ago, the dissenting voice is drowned in the clamour of the organised caucus.

EMMA. Listen to you! (*Pause: quietly.*) Come on. Take me upstairs. (*Pause.*) Fuck me then. (*Pause.*) Could you?

JOHN (*sitting*). Emma. It's the oldest trick in the world to make specious comparisons between sexuality and politics.(*Pause.*) You didn't put the black shirt on me – so to speak – when I had you in the bathroom this morning.

EMMA. No. And you didn't come, either.

JOHN. Do you care?

EMMA (*shouting*). No!

Pause.

JOHN. Dear me. I think we'd better go upstairs after all.

EMMA. There isn't time.

This gets a triumphant grin. He gets up stretching and yawning.

EMMA. You bastard!

JOHN. What a day. Three hernias, two hysterectomies and the poet's gall-stones. (*Pause.*) To be rounded off so rivetingly by dinner with your brother's wife. (*Pause.*) I wonder if she'll bring that astonishing dog with her again. Looks like an earwig. (*Pause.*) I hope you won't preach, Emma. Or go on about the Palestinians. Or Zionism. You'll only convince her you're an anti-semite. (*Drinks.*) Robert's frightened her out of her wits on that subject already. (*Pause.*) We could try asking

her what she thinks about monetarism and the male orgasm.
Would that be safe?

Pause.

EMMA. Why did you ask Robert to look her up in Rome?

JOHN. Who?

EMMA. Isabel.

Pause.

JOHN. He told you? (*Pause.*) I thought she'd be awfully good
for him. Them. He and Esther need a third party. Shake 'em
up a bit.

EMMA. Well I told Robert. To tell her. Isabel. That if she's still
in Rome when you arrive tomorrow — I shall cut your throat
with one of your own scalpels when you get back.

EMMA *exits.* JOHN *thoughtfully addresses the door.*

JOHN. And what makes you think I'm coming back to you?

Scene Two

An apartment in Rome. Evening, the same day.
  *EMMA's brother ROBERT is pouring a drink. He is in his
mid-twenties.*
  ISABEL, now fifty-one, enters in a long robe.
  Bells toll softly outside.

ISABEL. Was that nice, Robert?

ROBERT. Great. (*Pause.*) I have an idea you didn't come, though.

Pause.

ISABEL. Well I nearly did.

*She goes to a tape deck and presses a button. The Mozart horn
concerto of the previous scene. ROBERT gives her a drink
and they sit.*

ROBERT. Lovely to know you, Isabel.

ISABEL. You too.

ROBERT (*listening*). That concerto —

ISABEL. Yes. It's one of John's favourites.

Pause.

ROBERT. It's still going on then?

ISABEL. I haven't seen him since he did my womb.

Pause.

ROBERT. What's it like without a womb?

ISABEL. Bliss.

ROBERT. Funny to think of John doing it.

ISABEL. It gave him an odd feeling too, he said.

ROBERT. A bit unethical, I'd have thought.

ISABEL. John says the rule is: your mistress can be your patient, but your patient mustn't become your mistress.

ROBERT. These doctors!

ISABEL. He's a fine surgeon.

Pause.

ROBERT. You'll have noticed his hands, I should imagine. (*Pause.*) In your dual mistress/patient role —

ISABEL. Don't sulk, darling.

Pause.

ROBERT. Those short stubby hairy navvy's fingers.

ISABEL. Very sexy they are.

ROBERT. I wouldn't let him examine my wife.

ISABEL. Does she need examining?

ROBERT. Seeing a gynaecologist is the nearest she ever gets to an erotic impulse.

Pause.

ISABEL. I was once on a dig with her father, you know. In Tunisia. (*Pause.*) A breathless girl Esther, he said. As if she'd been running ever since she was born.

ROBERT. Funny to think of you scrabbling about in ruins.

ISABEL. That's exactly the way I used to feel about John and his women patients.

Pause.

ROBERT. She has this dog, now. Esther has.

ISABEL. Still running.

ROBERT. For a girl who grew up in the sixties, she's a bit creepy.

ISABEL. How?

ROBERT. Well she was a virgin for one thing. And —

ISABEL. Perhaps virginity's coming back.

ROBERT. Yes. But at twenty-five? And in the seventies?

ISABEL. In my opinion, a lot of young people are reacting
   nowadays.

ROBERT. Against what?

ISABEL. Against the sixties, of course.

ROBERT. The point I'm trying to make. Is that Esther went on
   being a virgin in the sixties.

ISABEL. I see. You can't make up your mind whether she was
   heroic or retarded. (*Pause.*) I'll bet you were secretly pleased,
   though. When you finally had her.

ROBERT. She didn't stay a virgin for me. She didn't know me till
   seventy-five.

ISABEL. And you think that's what led to the dog?

   ROBERT *crosses to stand looking out of the window.*

ROBERT. I don't know how you can live in Rome. (*Pause.*) One
   way and another.

ISABEL. Well, it's only a pied-à-terre really. And who'd want to
   kidnap me? Or shoot my sweet little kneecaps off?

ROBERT. Italy's a bit frightening, though.

ISABEL. I thought you were on Emma's side.

ROBERT. Emma's side of what?

ISABEL. Well isn't she a Eurocommunist or something?

ROBERT. What do you know about it?

ISABEL. Well I read the papers. I see what's going on. (*Pause.*)
   Have I got the wrong end of the ideological stick, vis-à-vis
   Emma?

ROBERT. I'll say you have. Emma regards Eurocommunism
   as the foulest revisionism. (*Pause.*) Which it is, really.

ISABEL. So where do your sympathies lie, darling? John told me
   you rather admire your sister.

ROBERT. Oh I do. Marginally. (*Pause.*) But for the time being —
   and in the absence of a revolutionary momentum in the
   working class — the British problem is the money supply.
   Pause.

ISABEL. I'm afraid you've lost me there.

ROBERT. Ask John when he gets here. (*Goes to refill his glass.*) He's an expansionist. (*Pause.*) More booze?

ISABEL. Yes please.

ROBERT (*bringing the bottle*). That was some fuck, Isabel.

ISABEL. Love-making's the only time I rather miss having a womb, to tell you the truth.

ROBERT. Is it all that different?

Pause.

ISABEL. One thinks of all those quaint little spermatozoa coming to a dead end.

ROBERT. I'll bet the thought's crossed old John's mind, as well.

ISABEL. Don't sulk, darling.

ROBERT. I loathe and detest that bloody horn concerto.

ISABEL. It goes everywhere with me.

ROBERT. You know. Psychologically speaking. (*Sits.*) You do come across as belonging to another epoch, Isabel.

ISABEL. Never mind. I'm sure my epoch's on its way in again too. Hand in hand with virginity. (*Pause.*) You see that little figurine over there? (*He looks.*) Over there?

ROBERT. What about it?

ISABEL. It's Mycenean. (*Pause.*) They were civilised when Enrico Berlinguer's ancestors were toddling about in furs.

Pause.

ROBERT. I wonder why you never married John?

ISABEL. You shouldn't wonder. Speculation coarsens the mind.

Pause.

ROBERT. Needless to say, it doesn't follow that if one's a monetarist one can have no truck with expansion.

ISABEL. My Uncle Percy never saw eye to eye with Keynes. (*Pause.*) He said: if the demented feller really thinks we can move the economy by paying chaps to dig holes — then the first one should be a nice deep grave for Mr Keynes himself.

Pause.

ROBERT. I keep thinking of Esther's bloody dog.

ISABEL. Why did I let you into my bed? I knew at once

you're the type that gets introspective after orgasm. (*Pause.*)
And I don't make a habit of it, you know.

ROBERT You had my friend Edouard at the Sorbonne, eleven
years ago.

ISABEL. I don't recollect having him at the Sorbonne.

ROBERT. You know what I mean, Isabel.

ISABEL. One had to do something for the boys of Paris '68.

ROBERT. I saw Edouard in Paris the other day. He said by the
autumn of sixty-eight your Rome apartment was the only
building still left occupied in the French revolution.

ISABEL. That was a golden year, all right.

Pause.

ROBERT. I don't know why. But it's very hard to forgive older
women their promiscuity.

ISABEL. All smelly and bruised, he was. He had fifteen stitches
in his scalp. A frightful wound from a gendarme's baton.

ROBERT. Europe nearly fell, Isabel.

ISABEL. Well it's been staggering long enough.

ROBERT. They'd have known what to do with people like
John Baildon, I can tell you.

ISABEL. Then it's just as well De Gaulle knew what to do with
them.

ROBERT. I might have known you'd turn out a reactionary
bitch.

ISABEL. Darling. Sex had just the same effect on Edouard. As
soon as it was over he was up on the barricades screaming
down at me again. Sexist! Bourgeois! (*Pause.*) That's the kind
of talk women hear from a certain type of young revolutionary.
They seem to think cant and cunt are words stemming from
the same root.

Pause.

ROBERT. Well I don't see how you can keep on with John now.

ISABEL. You're not dragging an affaire out of me you know.
(*Pause.*) Not one of those with an 'e' like the French. (*Pause.*)
Let me put it this way. (*She crosses to get a drink, but stops
and touches his cheek.*) You walked in through that door, and
I had you. I had you because you were there and I was feeling

like it. (*Going to the drinks.*) You aren't just any old bit of trash out of nowhere. (*Smiles, pouring.*) John will be fascinated. Don't look so crestfallen. It'll send you up in his estimation. (*Pause.*) A little. (*Pause.*) Ten out of ten for sheer nerve, anyway. He likes nerve. (*Stands looking out.*) I sometimes have the feeling your generation thinks it invented sexual liberation. (*Drinks.*) Why don't you go home and kill your wife's dog?

ROBERT. Why doesn't your class and generation stop hiding behind cheap cynicism?

Pause.

ISABEL. My — class, did you say Robert?

ROBERT. Yes. And don't give me any shit about its having become a meaningless term these days. I've heard it all ad nauseam from my parents.

ISABEL. And what might their class predicament be?

ROBERT. Upper middle, not to mess about with definitions.

ISABEL. How you must have suffered.

ROBERT (*going to the door*). I'm sorry I didn't come up to your expectations.

ISABEL. How could I have any when I didn't know you were coming to see me?

She coaxes him back by the arm and refills his glass.

I'd hate you to go away feeling wounded.

ROBERT (*shouting*). I'm not feeling wounded.

Pause.

ISABEL. How long did you say you'd be in Rome?

ROBERT. A week.

ISABEL. John's only staying two days.

Pause. He sips his drink, looking at her.

ROBERT. He and Emma aren't getting on at all well, you know.

ISABEL. What a pity. His background's impeccably working-class.

Pause.

ROBERT. I know I talk a lot of shit myself, Isabel.

ISABEL. Only since you got out of bed, darling.

ROBERT. It didn't help listening to John's favourite horn
   concerto, I can tell you.

ISABEL. Robert —

ROBERT. What?

ISABEL. Do sit down.

   He does so. She sits opposite.

ISABEL. I want you to know. I consider it an insult for a person
   to define me in terms of class, generation or profession.

ROBERT. There you are. A typical bourgeois!

ISABEL. I am an individual, Robert.

ROBERT. Classical.

ISABEL. I imagine as far as communism's concerned, you're one
   of those who tend to travel aimlessly rather than arrive.

ROBERT. Perhaps. (*Pause.*) But —

ISABEL. Could it be that Esther's repelled by your foreskin?

ROBERT. Now look here, Isabel —

ISABEL. Shall I bite it off?

   Pause.

ROBERT. Wow!

   Pause.

ISABEL (*leans back, smiling*). I wish you could see your face.

ROBERT. Why?

ISABEL. I've never seen such a piggy, lustful little face.

   ROBERT *starts pulling his jacket off.*

ISABEL (*rising*). Then we'll have a lovely dinner. And you can
   tell me all I want to know about your sister.

Scene Three

ISABEL's *apartment the following afternoon.*
   JOHN *and* ISABEL *enter together.*

JOHN. All I can say is: Millington may be a world authority on
   cancer of the cervix, but it didn't prevent the entire
   conference falling asleep. (*Slumps into a chair.*) Whew.

ISABEL. Drink?

JOHN. Yes please.

She goes to get the drinks.

JOHN. Lovely to see you, Isabel.

ISABEL. You too.

JOHN. Innards all right?

ISABEL. Yes thank you. (*Pause.*) After all it's two years.

JOHN. My God so it is.

ISABEL. The day before you and Emma got married. (*Pause.*)
   I only got back from Brazil last week.

JOHN. Well. You look very brown and beautiful.

ISABEL. Thank you.

JOHN. Give me a stunner, will you?

*He gets up and wanders to the tape deck. Pushes a button. The
Mozart horn concerto.*

JOHN. Isabel!

ISABEL. I was playing it only yesterday.

She brings the drinks to a table.

JOHN. My wife has a most peculiar reaction to this horn concerto.

ISABEL. Her brother doesn't seem to like it much either.

He looks at her reproachfully as she proffers his drink.

JOHN. Isabel!

ISABEL. Cheers (*Drinks.*) Yes. I had him yesterday.

JOHN. Cheers. (*Drinks.*) I'm extremely huffed.

ISABEL. Liar.

JOHN. Was he any good?

ISABEL. A bit orthodox. (*Pause.*) I rather think he needed a
   shiksa. After a few years with Esther.

Pause.

JOHN (*sitting*). He's got a bee in his bonnet about the money
   supply, you know.

ISABEL. He says you have one about expansion.

Pause.

JOHN. What on earth are you going to do with him?

ISABEL. I think I've done most of it.

JOHN. Isabel!

ISABEL. It's your fault. I've been a randy old bag since you did my hysterectomy.

Pause.

JOHN. Would you believe it. I think I'm vaguely in love with Robert's wife. (*Pause.*) I haven't declared myself.

ISABEL. I hope it won't interfere with Haiti.

JOHN. Absolutely not. Haiti's in the bag. All one has to do with Emma is harp on about it. After a week you can hear her screaming No from the other side of Regents Park. (*Pause.*) We had dinner with Esther last night.

ISABEL. Robert's very worried about her.

JOHN. She's doggedly hysterical about him.

ISABEL. And how's Emma?

JOHN. It turns out she's wildly jealous about you.

ISABEL. But you and I haven't —

JOHN. I mean, that you're still alive.

Pause.

ISABEL. Robert did say she's immature, that's all.

JOHN. It's quite enough.

ISABEL. It's a bit much. When we haven't since before you did my womb.

JOHN. Well by her reckoning you ought to be dead by now.

ISABEL. I'm younger than you.

JOHN. Men don't count.

Pause.

ISABEL. I sometimes wonder if you weren't a bit over-eager to get my insides out.

JOHN. Oh, Emma doesn't know you've got any actual parts missing. She just assumes you've been depreciating over the years. Misfiring occasionally. And —

ISABEL. I'm not a bloody motor car.

JOHN. I never told her I had to snick a few bits out of you, here and there.

ISABEL. Nor did you tell me it would turn me from an ordinary whore into a genuine nymphomaniac.

JOHN. Dear old Isabel.

ISABEL. When I got your letter with that lovely plot for two weeks in Haiti, I was in a rain forest. (*Pause.*) All the way in a dugout canoe, your letter came.

JOHN. Paddled by sturdy Indians?

ISABEL. They all seem to have outboard motors, nowadays.

JOHN. Makes you think. Doesn't it? (*Pause.*) Did you find any jolly ruins?

ISABEL. A cranky theory of Esther's father's, as it happens. (*Pause.*) I think I've proved him wrong.

JOHN. Aztec gold?

ISABEL. You're still charmingly adolescent and romantic, John.

JOHN. Well I'm glad you think so, because —

ISABEL. Of course in one sense it's despicable to go to Haiti.

Pause.

JOHN. Because I was thinking of switching to Esther for Haiti.

Pause.

ISABEL. Well that takes a load off my mind.

JOHN. I thought there might be a row.

ISABEL. We've never had a row.

Pause.

JOHN. I can't get that damned dog of hers out of my mind.

ISABEL. Esther sounds quite middle-aged, somehow.

JOHN. You've put your finger on it. (*Pause.*) A lot of them are nowadays.

ISABEL (*crossing to window*). I'm thinking of becoming a Catholic. (*Pause.*) And that's quite enough, without gallivanting off to Haiti.

JOHN. I always knew something serious would happen to you one day, Isabel.

ISABEL *turns slowly to look at him.*

ISABEL. You were my serious thing.

Pause.

JOHN. A light inconsequential affair like ours?

ISABEL. It was never that to me.

Pause.

JOHN. But — so long ago.

ISABEL. You've always kept in touch.

JOHN. And I've always been a featherweight in love, Isabel.

ISABEL. That's something for your conscience, not mine.

Pause.

JOHN. Conscience?

She brings the bottle over.

ISABEL. I mean, I didn't love you according to the strength or weakness of your own feelings. (*Pause.*) I decided it would never do to let you know how much I loved you. (*Smiles.*) You've always been afraid of depth, my dear. (*Pouring.*) You're not a superficial man. But you will posture. And challenge people to take it or leave it. (*Pause.*) So I thought I'd better leave you to less discerning women.

Pause.

JOHN. Could you have picked up some sort of virus, in the Orinoco Basin?

ISABEL. The Orinoco's Venezuela, darling. (*Pause.*) But do you know what? There I was one evening a few weeks ago. Sitting on the terrace of a little hotel somewhere up the Amazon. And I heard one of those old mechanical gramophones playing a Vera Lynn record. (*Pause.*) Oh, it did take me back.

JOHN. Yes. I suppose it would. (*Pause.*) Funny, how the end of the war seems just last week. Isn't it? (*Pause.*) The other day, really. (*Pause.*) There's no doubt about it. She was the Maria Callas of light entertainment.

ISABEL. You're not coming into my bed, you know.

JOHN. Have I been usurped by Robert? Or by God?

ISABEL (*sitting*). My faith is immune to irony, sarcasm or insult. (*Smiling.*) It's impregnable.

JOHN. So was your uterus. Did I ever tell you? Like a dried sponge.

Pause.

ISABEL. I went on playing the same old game with you for a while this time, because I wanted to disarm you. (*Sipping.*) Lead you on a bit.

JOHN. Oh yes?

ISABEL. What you'd like. Is for me to take care of Robert if you do get his wife to Haiti. Wouldn't you?

JOHN. Now that is a bit far-fetched.

ISABEL. When were your schemes ever plausible?

Pause.

JOHN. I must say. The prospect of eternal life doesn't seem to have blunted your wits.

ISABEL. Your trouble is that you believe in people staying married, however promiscuous they are.

JOHN. Don't you think it's a great deal more convenient that way?

Pause.

ISABEL. I gave Robert the screwing of his life, yesterday.

JOHN. Let's hope Esther profits by it.

ISABEL. I knew that was what you wanted.

JOHN. One last act of malice?

ISABEL. Charity.

JOHN. I can see you're filled with inner radiance, Isabel. Sticks out a mile. (*Pause.*) Mucking about on some higher plane altogether. (*Drinks.*) You were much nicer when you were down here in the shit with the rest of us.

ISABEL. What's your wife got against Mozart?

JOHN. Her new political convictions have forced her to reappraise everything. Drama to start with of course. I mean — she left the theatre, albeit in the nick of time. To work for this improbable party of hers. And then —

ISABEL (*softly*). Was Chekhov her hero too?

Pause.

JOHN. Then literature became insipid, and painting irrelevant. A load of elitist crap, you might say. (*Pause.*) Now music's down the drain as well. She's really got it in for old Wolfgang Amadeus. (*Drinks.*) It transforms them you know, this revolutionary passion. Changes their entire perspective.

(*Pause.*) I don't know her. She's a stránger. If it weren't for my lust and my income she'd walk out I'm sure. No kidding Just like that. (*Drinks.*) That's what our marriage has become. Two absolute strangers dangling resentfully from the same prick.

Pause.

ISABEL. My lover is a writer. I used to say to the mirror. (*Pause.*) My lover will be the Chekhov of the Fifties.

Pause.

JOHN. Won't you even consider fellatio? For auld lang syne?

ISABEL. I don't think so, John darling. The shock I administered to Robert yesterday was my swan song.

JOHN. Should I be getting along, then?

ISABEL. Oh, stay a bit.

Pause.

JOHN. I took some gall-stones out of a poet, yesterday morning. (*Pause.*) Merry little chap.

ISABEL. They were inscribed: ante omnia verbum.

JOHN. What?

Pause.

TOGETHER. In the beginning was the word.

He pours himself a drink and goes to the window.

JOHN. I feel like getting absolutely plastered. (*Pause.*) The thing is, you know. I don't confine myself to pouring scorn on Emma's political beliefs. I'm cruel about them. (*Pause.*) She and her friends can't tolerate the unconverted. And their sense of rectitude drives me to apoplexy. (*Turns, smiling.*) Which I hide, of course. (*Pause.*) I become the coldly smiling adversary. I use unfair tactics. I try to destroy her confidence in every way. (*Drinks.*) Then even more barbarous methods occur to me. (*Drinks.*) I held Esther's ankle between mine for twenty minutes last night. Under the table. At dinner with Emma beside me. (*Pause.*) Until —

Pause.

ISABEL. Yes?

JOHN. The bloody dachshund bit me.

ISABEL. I never could stay angry with you for long.

JOHN. I'm glad you're not miffed about Haiti.

ISABEL (*raising her glass*). Down with Baby Doc.

JOHN. Down with Baby Doc.

They look at each other. She crosses to him and kisses his cheek lightly. She looks out of the window.

ISABEL. I love the autumn light in Rome.

JOHN. When you came towards me at the fountain, I thought you walked in light.

ISABEL. I could never settle down in England again.

JOHN. Do people sneer much, Isabel?

ISABEL. About my conversion?

JOHN. Yes.

ISABEL. I haven't told anyone.

JOHN. I thought maybe — some of the old lot, you know.

ISABEL. I never see the 'old lot'.

She goes to sit down. He sits opposite.

JOHN. There was a time when I could make you do anything I wanted.

Pause.

ISABEL (*quietly*). So long ago.

Pause.

JOHN. You did everything. You were my exclusive whore. (*Pause.*) You were magnificent, Isabel.

ISABEL. In those days. (*Pause.*) For you.

Pause.

JOHN. But once you were past a certain age —

ISABEL. Oh yes. (*Pause.*) Your women have got younger and younger, over the years. (*Shouting.*) But I was your youngest!

She starts sobbing, shaking violently. JOHN *relaxes. He lights a cigarette. Leans back in his chair looking at her. Slowly she regains control. Pours herself a drink. The bottle rattles loudly against the rim of the glass.*

JOHN (*coldly*). Why God? (*Pause.*) What's wrong with middle-aged depravity? (*Pause.*) Aren't you rather insulting your own intelligence?

Pause.

ISABEL. What on earth has intelligence . . . to do with religious faith?

JOHN. Absolutely nothing, I'm sure. Which is precisely my point. The two simply don't go together. Chalk and cheese. How disgusting to utter the two concepts in the same breath! (*Pause.*) But I didn't come to Rome to be dragged into some naive theological debate, Isabel darling.

Pause.

ISABEL. You sent Robert ahead. (*Pause.*) Like a scout.

JOHN (*standing*). Robert's function. (*Pause.*) Well you know. Let me put it this way. (*Pause.*) I assumed you must have become pretty stagnant, this past two years. (*Pause.*) Shall we say Robert's function was to clean the scum off the pond? (*Pause.*) I really didn't think I could waste too much time restoring the status quo ante. (*Refills his glass.*) I won't say it's pure fantasy about Esther, but I did see Robert more by way of getting you in shape. (*Drinks.*) Preparing you for me. (*Drinks.*) I looked at Robert one day last week and I thought: well you're young. You're not grotesquely ill-mannered. You can bloody well drop in on old Isabel in Rome and do some spade-work for a change. (*Drinks.*) Who won?

Pause.

ISABEL. It was I who had the upper hand yesterday.

JOHN. Doubtless because you took the wise precaution of tiring him out first.

Pause.

ISABEL. Go away, John.

JOHN. Damned if I will.

ISABEL (*shouting*). Get out of here!

JOHN. Isabel. Don't you think it's a little vulgar to embark on your relationship with God by opting for sexual continence with me? (*Pause.*) Isn't that old hat, from a theological point of view? Isn't it just a bit of moral tat? (*Drinks.*) Cook up any sort of rational arguments you like, but sod throwing the towel in to divine intervention.

Pause.

ISABEL (*very quietly*). I . . . I do have the sense . . . of a small . . . flickering light . . . somewhere inside me.

JOHN. Where inside you? (*Pause.*) On the tomb of the unknown soldier?

Pause.

ISABEL. A tiny flame of belief.

JOHN. Dear me. My wife has one of those. What do you think you are — a couple of bloody lanterns?

He drains his glass and goes to sit beside her. She gets up and backs away. He parts his legs slightly.

ISABEL. No!

Pause.

JOHN. Oh yes you will.

Pause.

ISABEL. I can't.

There is a long silence. They are staring at each other. ISABEL kneels in front of him. He takes her head in his hands. She moves forward between his thighs and begins to unzip him.

Scene Four

ISABEL's *apartment. Late the following night.*
     ISABEL *sits drinking whiskey, a bottle and glass beside her on a table.*
     The doorbell rings. Then twice more. She makes her way rather unsteadily across the room and goes out. She comes back with ROBERT.

ISABEL. I'm rather pissed, I'm afraid.

ROBERT. He's gone back to London?

ISABEL. This afternoon.

ROBERT. I'm none too sober myself.

ISABEL pours the last of the whiskey into her glass.

ISABEL. There's another bottle over there. Will you get it?

He goes to fetch the bottle and another glass.

ROBERT. There's an odd sort of smell in here.

ISABEL. Is there?

Pause.

ROBERT. A sort of — rutting smell. (*Pause.*) Kleenex and dried semen.

ISABEL. Ah, how the nostalgic memories of Harrow come rushing back!

Pause.

ROBERT. Bedales.

ISABEL. Emma too?

ROBERT. Emma too.

Pause.

ISABEL. Did you run into a Jesuit on the stairs?

ROBERT. How would I have known it was a Jesuit?

ISABEL. He'd have been wearing a black shirt, jeans and sneakers. (*Pause.*) And a tin badge with Snoopy in a flying helmet.

ROBERT. I thought you were having me on, about God.

ISABEL. I didn't let him in. I mean the Jesuit, of course.

He sits. They drink.

ISABEL. Does your sister give the impression of having a small, flickering light inside her?

ROBERT. It's not the sort of thing one looks for in a sister.

ISABEL. But she is a fanatical revolutionary.

ROBERT. It doesn't produce the effect of inward illumination.

ISABEL. You should be more loyal.

ROBERT. Oh, I'm loyal. But from a purely intellectual point of view, I'd say there's more fog than light in the girl. (*Drinks.*) Ideologically speaking, she's a pea-souper.

Pause.

ISABEL. I don't know why on earth you young people go on getting married at all.

ROBERT. Isabel I've been wanting you ever since I left you —

ISABEL. God knows why I let you in and kept the Jesuit on the other side of the door.

ROBERT. I'm serious, Isabel.

ISABEL. I wrote him a note and pushed it out to him.

Pause.

ROBERT. Saying what?

ISABEL. Saying the whole thing's a crock of shit.

ROBERT. Isn't that an American expression though?

ISABEL. He's an American Jesuit.

Pause.

ROBERT. You've changed since I last saw you.

ISABEL. You only think that because you're not panting at me through a tangle of arms and legs.

Pause.

ROBERT. You seem truly bitter, this evening. (*Pause.*) Or sad.

ISABEL. Robert you're a crock of shit yourself.

Pause.

ROBERT. What happened?

ISABEL. When?

ROBERT. With John.

She crosses to stand over him.

ISABEL. How old do you think I am?

ROBERT. Does it matter?

ISABEL. How drunk do you think I am?

ROBERT. Not very. (*Pause.*) Not really.

ISABEL. If that Mycenean figurine weren't too small and too precious. I'd split your skull with it.

Pause.

ROBERT. Emma says she actually does love him. (*Pause.*) John. (*Pause.*) It's weird.

ISABEL. Why not? I should think he epitomises everything she's supposed to loathe. I wouldn't be surprised if she secretly adores him.

ROBERT. If our ages were reversed. Would you care?

ISABEL. If our ages were reversed. I wouldn't be wearing the bloody pious expression that's stuck on your face.

ROBERT. I resent it myself. It's habitual. It comes from having a neurotic wife and trying to take her ridiculous problems seriously. (*Pause.*) It's a muscular spasm. A psychological tic. It's the outcome of insincerity locked in a futile struggle

with compassion. (*He stands facing her.*) You shouldn't
try to humiliate me. You're just like my brother-in-law. You
hate young people. What's the matter with you all? (*Drinks.*)
At least I keep my piety on my face, which is all it's fit for.
(*Pause.*) How have you dissembled all your life? With your
cunt?

*She slaps his face hard. His glass goes spinning off across the
room. She goes to the window.* ROBERT *finds another
glass and pours himself a stiff drink.*

ROBERT. Well. I'm not pretending to walk out this time. (*Drinks.*)
I'm glad it's the Jesuits who've got you. At least a few of
them have minds. (*Drinks.*) Meanwhile you can get into that
bloody bedroom.

Pause.

ISABEL. We — hate young people? (*Pause.*) John and I?

Pause.

ROBERT. That perverse man is cutting my sister to pieces.
With smiling dexterity.

ISABEL. And what do you use on Esther? A blunt instrument?

ROBERT *sits slumped forward over his knees, turning the
glass between his fingers.*

ROBERT. What did you use on me the other day? (*Pause.*) I
hadn't thought of myself as inexperienced. But you made me
feel as if I'd been a child before. (*Pause.*) An innocent.
(*Pause: shouts.*) That was cannibalism!

Pause.

ISABEL. But you can't wait for more. (*Pause.*) Can you?

ROBERT. When I got back to my hotel I went straight to the
bar and stayed there for hours. (*Pause.*) I was shocked.
Euphoric. I was shocked at being shocked. (*Pause.*) Then I
wanted to get back here. (*Pause.*) There's a little balcony
outside my room. I stood there for a bit. There was a riot
going on somewhere. Police. Sirens. Shooting. Ambulances.
Tear gas shells exploding. (*Pause.*) I thought: this world's
disintegrating. And I wanted to run to you. (*Pause.*) Rome
was hellish, all of a sudden. (*Pause.*) One thing you can say
about the young. We don't own this world. It isn't ours.
(*Pause.*) I don't think we stand a chance.

Pause.

ISABEL. We once did think it was ours.

Pause.

ROBERT. Marx should never have called history a midwife.
It's an abortionist.

Pause. ISABEL *crosses to him. Touches his cheek.*

ISABEL. Ah, Robert.

ROBERT. I feel naive and callow. All in the head. (*Pause.*) I
almost envy my sister. She can't tell an axiom from a
platitude — but she has a passionate sense of justice.
(*Pause.*) I'll go now. Really. (*He smiles.*) Hadn't you better
give your Jesuit a ring?

But he doesn't move. ISABEL *turns away from him coming
downstage. A silence.*

ROBERT. Charlie Brown for Pope?

Pause.

ISABEL. Funny how the war seems like just the other day.

Pause.

ROBERT. I love Emma very much. (*Pause.*) I don't know how she
and John —

ISABEL. The first time John and I made love was VE Day. May
nineteen forty-five. (*Pause.*) He was a young captain, on leave
from Germany. (*Pause.*) I was seventeen. (*Pause.*) People
were singing and dancing in the streets — wild with joy.
(*Pause.*) He'd managed to get us a room at Claridge's of all
places. (*Pause.*) I watched him afterwards, lying there smoking.
And smiling. (*Pause.*) What are you grinning at, I said. (*Pause.*)
I was just thinking, he said. Here am I a Yorkshire miner's
son, in bed with a peer's niece in bloody Claridge's! (*Pours
a drink.*) He took my face in his hands. (*Pause.*) By Christ
things are going to be different this time, he said. (*Pause.*)
And we — what shall I say? (*Pause.*) Cannibalised each other
all night.

ROBERT (*standing*). Well. How interestingly you've both
fulfilled that first blush of promise!

Pause.

ISABEL. There wasn't meant to be a moral to the story.

ROBERT. What then?

Pause.

ISABEL. After what you just said about Rome. (*Pause.*) And

thinking back on that night in London years ago.
(*Pause.*) I felt such a stab of pity.

Pause.

ROBERT. For anyone or anything in particular?

ISABEL. John and I, we —

ROBERT (*going to the door. He stops and turns*). Yes?

   Pause.

ISABEL. Nothing. (*Pause.*) Absolutely nothing.

   He goes out. After a moment ISABEL *picks up the figurine.
   She stands looking at it, and slowly drains her glass.*

Scene Five

The sitting-room of JOHN BAILDON's *house in London. Late
afternoon the following day.*
   EMMA *sits in the chair used by* JOHN *in Scene One.*
   JOHN *enters carrying a briefcase which he drops on the floor.*

JOHN. Hello, Trotters.

EMMA. Hello.

   He approaches her from behind and kisses the top of her head.

JOHN. Welcome home, John.

EMMA. Welcome home, John.

JOHN (*crossing to pour drinks*). Would you say that Heathrow
   Airport was consciously designed to be the dreariest in
   Europe? (*Brings her drink.*) A grubby inconvenient muddle
   full of grubby inconvenient people. (*Sits.*) Let's get it cleared
   up straight away, I said to the passport officer. (*Drinks.*) I'm
   not a virgin.

EMMA. Oh yes.

JOHN. Yes. I got one of those weary English smiles they're so
   good at.

EMMA. I expected you yesterday.

JOHN. God knows why they put tanks round it in seventy-four.
   I should think your average revolutionary wouldn't be seen
   dead there. (*Drinks.*) Not without a first class ticket and VIP
   status.

EMMA. Like we-know-who.

Pause.

JOHN. I stopped overnight in Paris. With Millie-the-cervix and his wife. Riveting chap. I shouldn't think they need an anaesthetist when he's in the theatre. (*Pause.*) Phoned you several times. No reply. (*Pause.*) Haranguing the workers down at the latest picket-line, were we?

EMMA. I was out with Esther.

JOHN. I wish you'd lay off her. She wasn't personally responsible for the creation of Israel, you know.

EMMA. She killed her dog.

JOHN. The little brute.

EMMA. It was an accident.

JOHN. I meant — the dog.

EMMA. Backed the car over it.

JOHN. And the silly bugger let her?

EMMA. One of its paws was caught in a drain.

JOHN. Well. At least we can all now sleep soundly in our beds.

EMMA. I don't know what it ever did to you.

JOHN. It bloody well nipped my ankle. That's what it did. (*Pause.*) More than once.

EMMA. They don't like strange men playing footsie with their mistresses.

JOHN. When's the funeral?

EMMA. And talking of corpses. How's that hag of yours in Rome?

Pause.

JOHN. Ah yes. My hag. (*Drinks.*) Poor old bag. She's fine, thank you.

EMMA. Robert rang Esther from Rome the other night. (*Pause.*) Drunk. (*Pause.*) He said the thing he had going with your old flame made his and Esther's sex life seem like a chronic display of chastity.

JOHN. It seems Isabel's having a last fling or two before she embraces the Roman Catholic Church.

EMMA. Sounds as if she's flung Robert some considerable distance.

JOHN. And it would be the day after that when Esther — inadvertently of course — slew little Bongo?

EMMA. Better than reversing the car over Robert.

JOHN. You've hit the nail on the head there, Emma. (*Pause.*) I wondered whether Bongo knew he was little more than a small, intemperate, frankfurter-shaped substitute for your brother.

Pause.

EMMA. I've been taking a beady look at our marriage whilst you were away.

JOHN. Good Lord yes! Why not? Does it still show?

Pause.

EMMA. I thought we might have a baby.

Pause.

JOHN. I'd rather have a Bongo.

Pause.

EMMA. I've often wondered. Why you and your first wife didn't have a child. (*Pause.*) Things being so dodgy between you.

Pause.

JOHN. I think. Because it would have been. Little more than a small, intemperate, frankfurter-shaped substitute for me.

Pause.

EMMA. Why did the Nazis send her father to Dachau?

JOHN. He was a communist, Emma.

EMMA. And you rail against me!

Pause.

JOHN. Her mother disappeared in a Russian labour camp after the war.

EMMA. I don't defend the Soviet Union. On the contrary. I —

JOHN. My mother-in-law — as she would have been — was a communist too, Emma. (*Pause.*) One is always the wrong kind of communist for somebody.

EMMA. Do you think I haven't done my bloody homework?

JOHN. Well you brought up the subject. I've always carefully avoided it. (*Drinks.*) What with your irrationally acquired faith, and so on. (*Pause.*) Who am I to criticise an embryonic Rosa Luxemburg?

EMMA. You're a disgrace to the memory of your first wife's parents!

He crosses to her slowly. Stands looking at her.

JOHN. And in my opinion. You and your friends are a disgrace to the human moral intelligence.

He goes to fill his glass.

EMMA. I want to know what you were doing in Rome.

JOHN. Well, Manzini of Sienna chewed the fat about fallopian tube transplants for about sixteen hours. And —

EMMA. Exactly what you were doing, I mean.

Pause.

JOHN. It was all over between Isabel and me, long ago.

EMMA. Like — when?

JOHN. Like — in the early summer of forty-five.

EMMA. That's bullshit. She was your mistress for years.

Pause.

JOHN. None the less. That's when it was really over.

Pause.

EMMA. I want to know about it.

JOHN (*sits*). Someone at the War Office had me posted from Germany to the Far East in the summer of forty-five. (*Pause.*) Two atom bombs later, I ended up in Saigon. (*Pause.*) Curious. Because I was up for demobilisation.

EMMA. What for? Your bloody Victoria Cross?
at any rate.

Pause.

JOHN. I don't think whoever got me posted was impressed by it,

Pause.

EMMA. So?

Pause.

JOHN. Oh, I kept running into Isabel over the years.

EMMA. When you were with Gisele? (*Pause.*) Did she know?

Pause.

JOHN. Truly, Emma. I didn't destroy Gisele. (*Pause.*) She simply never developed from the small, shattered child I found on the streets in Marienborn. (*Pause.*) Ten years later I'd got over the war. (*Pause.*) She was still living it.

EMMA. I wonder what unholy impulse made you find her and

marry her. (*Pause.*) And ditch her so soon.

JOHN. Something drove me to it. (*Pause,*) What can one say about these enigmas?

EMMA. What drove little old Isabel?

Pause.

JOHN. She became quite a distinguished archaeologist. (*Pause.*) Well. As an old American friend of mine once said: Isabel may have her nose in the tombs, but she sure does keep her ass in the air. (*He goes to the window.*) She's a bit leathery now. (*Pause.*) Must be all that desert sun. And rooting about in the sand with people like Esther's father. (*Drinks.*) You only have to look at him to see he never got past the bucket and spade stage.

Pause.

EMMA. You're not telling me why you still have to see her.

JOHN (*smiling, turning*). We all have our secret humiliations. (*Pause.*) The heart's darkness.

EMMA. Is there something between you and her I could never forgive?

JOHN. We are hardly yours to judge.

EMMA. I meant — in the context of your marrying me.

Pause.

JOHN. Absolutely nothing at all, Emma. (*Pause.*) We were lucky enough to be spared a mediocre future together. (*Pause.*) We had three nights at Claridge's. (*Pause.*) That was all. (*Pause.*) At the time. (*Pause.*) I have a dim memory of her drinking champagne in bed. And saying — apropos the end of the war — thank God that's all over. (*Pause.*) Now we can get back to normal.

Pause.

EMMA. Stupid bitch.

JOHN. She was only seventeen.

EMMA (*shouting*). But you went on sleeping with her for years!

Pause.

JOHN. Now and then. (*Pause.*) Here and there. (*Pause.*) Just when the winds of archaeology and international conferences on surgery blew us together. (*Pause.*) Paris. Stockholm. New York. Cairo. Lima. (*Pause.*) That sort of place.

He raises his glass, smiling at her over the rim. She leaps at him and knocks it out of his hand.

EMMA. Rome!

Pause.

JOHN. Sex is the most worn-out ideology of them all, Emma.

EMMA. Not for me it isn't!

Pause.

JOHN. Ah, you and me.

Pause.

EMMA. So what was so special between you and her?

JOHN. Sexually?

Pause.

EMMA. Maybe.

Pause.

JOHN. There isn't special sex, Emma. There are only special people.

EMMA. Well let's hope Isabel finds that God comes into that category.

Pause.

JOHN (*quietly*). Let's hope so.

She goes to switch on the tape deck (the Mozart). She fills their glasses and sits facing him. She takes a deep breath, bracing herself straight in the chair.

The phone rings. JOHN doesn't move. EMMA goes to answer it, switching off the tape.

EMMA. Emma Baildon —

There is a long silence as EMMA listens. She grows rigid.

EMMA. Oh, Esther. (*Pause.*) I'll ring you back.

She puts the phone down. Stands staring ahead.

JOHN. What was that about?

Pause.

EMMA. There was some demonstration or other in Rome. (*Pause.*) It got violent. (*Pause.*) And Robert —

JOHN. What would he be demonstrating about? He doesn't believe in anything.

She stands looking at him.

EMMA. He was just passing by,

JOHN. What's the betting he'd just been in bed with Isabel and was so bloody weak he couldn't run?

Pause.

EMMA (*quietly*). One of those long, glass-fronted arcades shattered. (*Pause: screaming.*) It's his eyes you bastard!

A silence. She sits. He watches her impassively.

EMMA. John. (*Pause.*) God I can't breathe. (*Pause: screaming.*) Jesus!

Pause.

JOHN. I'm sorry, Emma.

Pause.

EMMA. You're not! No you're not. (*Pause.*) And the way it happened.

JOHN. I'll bet the Italian equivalent of your lot was in there somewhere.

Pause.

EMMA. Just a bystander —

JOHN. Who isn't?

Sobbing, she goes to the door.

EMMA. I just wish —

Pause.

JOHN. What, Emma?

EMMA. I just wish somebody or something would strike you dead.

Pause.

JOHN. So do I.

She goes out. He lifts his glass slowly.

JOHN. So do I.

Curtain